Blockchain in Global Land Registries

Pablo L. Reiser · Michael Trübestein ·
Matthias Daniel Aepli

Blockchain in Global Land Registries

A Comparative Study of Blockchain-Based Land Registry Challenges

Springer Gabler

Pablo L. Reiser
University of Lucerne (HSLU)
Lucerne, Switzerland

Michael Trübestein
University of Lucerne (HSLU)
Lucerne, Switzerland

Matthias Daniel Aepli
University of Lucerne (HSLU)
Lucerne, Switzerland

ISBN 978-3-658-50075-7 ISBN 978-3-658-50076-4 (eBook)
https://doi.org/10.1007/978-3-658-50076-4

Gestaltung und Satz: Manuel Gächter, Oberegg
Lektorat/Planung: Guido Notthoff

This Springer Gabler imprint is published by the registered company Springer Fachmedien Wiesbaden GmbH, part of Springer Nature.
The registered company address is: Abraham-Lincoln-Str. 46, 65189 Wiesbaden, Germany

Management Summary

Land registries are supposed to provide clarity, reduce disputes, and act as trustworthy gatekeepers in property transactions. But in many parts of the world, they are doing the opposite. Paper-based processes, bureaucratic slowdowns, and legal uncertainty are still very much the norm. Even in countries with digital systems, many of these problems persist. Over the past decade, blockchain has been proposed as a fix: a way to add transparency, reduce fraud, and speed things up by removing the need for intermediaries. The promises are many. But what happens when theory meets practice? This thesis explores that question. While there is no shortage of writing on how blockchain *could* be used in land registries, much of it stays at the conceptual level. And when real-world pilot projects *are* mentioned, they are often glossed over or treated as proof-of-concept success stories without much detail on what actually went wrong, or right. In reality, the global picture is messier, and that is where this paper comes in. The goal here is not to rehash blockchain theory, but to look closely at how blockchain has actually been implemented (or at least attempted) in land administration systems across a few selected countries. Using a cross-case analysis of four key examples, Sweden, Georgia, Ghana, and India, this research tries to map out recurring roadblocks. What issues come up again and again? Which ones are specific to a country's legal framework, political setup, or infrastructure? And where have things gone right, if at all? The idea is to identify patterns, not just problems. By comparing these projects side by side, this thesis hopes to bring more clarity to what is holding blockchain back in this space and more importantly, what could help it move forward. Because while the tech itself is evolving fast, the same can't always be said for the systems trying to adopt it.

Keywords: Blockchain Technology, Land Administration, Land Registry, Digital Property Rights, Cross-Case Analysis, Implementation Barriers, Legal Frameworks, Public Sector Innovation

Table of Contents

List of Figures

List of Tables

1 Introduction

Property transactions are some of the most important and complex interactions a citizen can have with the state. At the heart of these interactions lies the land registry: the system that is supposed to record, verify, and protect land rights. But while the concept is simple, keep track of who owns what, the execution in reality is often not that simple. In many countries, land registries are slow, fragmented, and still largely paper based. Even where digital systems exist, they often replicate old workflows instead of replacing them. The result? Confusion, inefficiency, and in some cases, outright fraud.

Blockchain technology has been presented as a possible solution to these problems. By offering features like immutability, decentralization (or at least distributed trust), and transparency, blockchain promises to reduce the risk of manipulation, speed up transaction times, and improve public confidence in the system. Over the last few years, this idea has made its way from academic journals into pilot projects. Countries like Sweden, Georgia, Ghana, and India have all tested, in different ways, how blockchain might work in their land administration systems.

But despite all the attention and activity, full-scale adoption has not yet happened. Most projects remain stuck at the pilot stage, and in many cases, there is little clarity on why. What exactly went wrong? Was it the technology itself, or something deeper, like legal structures, institutional unwillingness to change, or social trust? While there is plenty of literature on blockchain's potential, very few studies take a grounded, comparative look at the practical experiences of these projects. That is the gap this research aims to fill.

Rather than building on abstract models, this research focuses on what has actually happened on the ground. Using a cross-case qualitative analysis,

P. L. Reiser et al., *Blockchain in Global Land Registries*,
https://doi.org/10.1007/978-3-658-50076-4_1

the thesis examines four blockchain-related initiatives in the land registry space, one each in Sweden, Georgia, Ghana, and India (Andhra Pradesh). These cases were selected based on the availability of detailed documentation and the diversity of their political, legal, and technical environments as well as their contribution to geographic variation. The method draws on the comparative logic of Miles et al. (2014), where the goal is not just to explain individual cases, but to identify recurring patterns and roadblocks that show up across jurisdictions.

The aim here is twofold. First, to map out the common challenges in implementing blockchain-based land registry systems. Second, to examine whether these barriers are case-specific or systemic. If similar problems keep showing up in different countries, then those problems may be structural and could be tackled in future designs. If they are unique, that also tells us something useful about the local limits of technological reform.

By pulling together the lessons from these four cases, this research aims to offer something that is often missing in the discussion: a practical, realistic view of what has been tried, what has failed, and where (if anywhere) the path forward might lie. The main structure of this thesis is to first lay out the theoretical background and case study summaries, then walk through the methodology of how the research will be carried out and finally present the findings from each case alongside the cross-case analysis.

2 Problem Statement

2

Property transfers have been around for centuries, but the systems used to manage them today, namely land registries, still lag behind. In many parts of the world, these systems are slow, heavily bureaucratic, and often paper based. What is meant to build trust between parties can end up doing the opposite: delays, inefficiencies, and even fraud are not uncommon. In the past decade or so, blockchain technology has been presented as a potential solution to these problems, offering transparency, immutability, and decentralized trust as some of its core features (Lemieux, 2016).

Several countries have tried to see what that might look like in practice. Sweden is probably the most well-known example, where a pilot project was carried out by the land agency (Lantmäteriet) to see whether property transactions could be done more efficiently using blockchain (*The Land Registry in the Blockchain*, 2016). Georgia also carried out a similar experiment with its National Agency of Public Registry, in collaboration with the private sector (Lazuashvili et al., 2019) as well as India (Thakur et al., 2020) and Ghana (Ameyaw, 2024) where this was also tried. All showed some promise but also faced issues that prevented full-scale implementation.

This is the core issue that this research aims to analyze. While there is no shortage of writing around how blockchain could work in land administration, a lot of it stays quite theoretical. On the other hand, when real-life projects are mentioned in papers talking about the theoretical potential of blockchain, they often get brushed over without much detail or follow-up. In the end, one is left with questions such as: when blockchain has been trialed in land registries, what actually happened? Why did a full-scale adoption not happen?

P. L. Reiser et al., *Blockchain in Global Land Registries*,
https://doi.org/10.1007/978-3-658-50076-4_2

From a research perspective, the absence of grounded, case-based studies makes it hard to build theory that actually reflects what is happening on the ground. From a practical perspective, it means countries and companies that want to innovate in this space are often starting from scratch, instead of building on previous learnings.

This research will therefore take a closer look at the cases where a pilot project aiming to introduce blockchain into land registries was carried out. By comparing them, the goal is to identify common roadblocks or bottlenecks, and to see whether these issues tend to repeat across different jurisdictions or if they are mainly tied to local legal, cultural, or technical factors. In doing so, this work hopes to bring more clarity to where the real challenges lie and what can be done to overcome or avoid them completely in future trials.

These real-world experiences are crucial to understand if future attempts are going to succeed, by allowing future trials to mitigate problems from the beginning. Otherwise, there is the risk of wasting time, effort, and resources on mistakes that others have already made.

3 Research Question

3

This research looks at the main problems that have come up in real-world projects trying to implement Blockchain technology into the land administration process. The focus is not on theory but on actual attempts that have been made in different countries through official pilot projects. Based on that, the main research question that guides this work is:

> **RQ1: "What are the common challenges in implementing blockchain-based land administration/registry systems, and what lessons can be learned from past cases?"**

Naturally, not all countries are the same. Some issues will likely be tied to a country's legal framework, political climate, or institutional setup. But the interesting part is to see whether there are problems that show up repeatedly, regardless of where exactly the project was carried out. If that turns out to be the case, then those might be the areas that need to be tackled first. If not, and most problems are case-specific, that also tells us something. To explore this angle further, a second question will be asked:

> **RQ2: "Are similar roadblocks to Blockchain implementation in land registries observable across jurisdictions?"**

To explore these questions, this thesis will rely on a cross-case analysis of selected blockchain implementation projects in land registries. This method was chosen because it makes it possible to compare and contrast multiple cases in a structured way. By doing so, the research can distinguish between problems that are context-specific and those that appear to be more widespread. It also allows for a better understanding of how different political, legal, and technological environments shape the outcomes of such projects.

P. L. Reiser et al., *Blockchain in Global Land Registries*,
https://doi.org/10.1007/978-3-658-50076-4_3

In addition to answering the questions above, this paper also has a few supporting goals. These are here to make sure the research is both useful in practice and clear to anyone reading it, even if they are not already familiar with blockchain or land administration. These objectives are:

- To explain the fundamentals of blockchain and land administration in simple terms.
- To go over past blockchain implementations in land registries, including ones that are still ongoing.
- To identify the main legal, technical, or institutional problems that have come up in these projects.

And finally, a note to the targeted audience. This research should hopefully be of use not just to academics, but also (and perhaps more importantly) to anyone working in or with land registries, policy makers looking to modernize systems, or developers building tech tools for government processes. If anything, the goal is to move the conversation forward by learning from what has already been done, instead of starting from zero every time.

4 Literature Review

Before diving into the core analysis, it is important to first set the stage and introduce the structure. This literature review is broken down into five main parts, each of which focuses on a different piece of the overall puzzle. It starts with a look at land administration systems, what they are, what they do, and why they matter. From there, a quick intro to blockchain fundamentals is provided to make sure the basics are clear for anyone who may not have a tech background. Particular focus was laid to ensure legibility and a non-technical explanation, so that the core concepts would be understandable. Then, the focus shifts to how land registries currently operate in most countries today, and some of the main problems that continue to come up. After that, the benefits are in theory: what blockchain could (in theory) bring to land administration, and where that promise starts to break down in practice. Finally, the literature review ends with an overview of the real-world case studies, places where blockchain has already been tested in land registries. Together, these five parts aim to build a full picture of the context this research is working within and help explain why the questions being asked here are worth exploring in the first place.

4.1 Land Administration Systems

For any functioning market a set of rules and rights need to be protected and administered in order to provide order and stability (UN-ECE, 1996). In the area of land and real estate this is done by a countries land administration department usually known as land registries. Though these two terms “Land Administration” and “Land Registration” are sometimes used interchangeably they do not work that way. Land administration is a broader term encompassing all functions of land management and tenure. Whereas

P. L. Reiser et al., *Blockchain in Global Land Registries*,
https://doi.org/10.1007/978-3-658-50076-4_4

land registration is a subset of land administration and one amongst a few others, these usually include:

1. Land Registration
2. Cadastral mapping
3. Land valuation and taxation
4. Land use planning and development control

Zevenbergen (2004) defines Land Registration as follows:

> *"Land registration is a process of official recording of rights in land through deeds or title (on properties). It means that there is an official record (the land register) of rights on land or of deeds concerning changes in the legal situation of defined units of land. It gives an answer to the question 'who' and 'how'."*

As for the Cadastral mapping he proposes the following definition:

> *"Cadastre is a methodically arranged public inventory of data concerning properties within a certain country or district, based on a survey of their boundaries. Such properties are systematically identified by means of some separate designation. The outlines or boundaries of the property and the parcel identifier are normally shown on large scale maps which, together with registers, may show for each separate property the nature, size, value and legal rights associated with the parcel. It gives an answer to the questions 'where' and 'how much'."*

A central reason why land registration systems exist is to bring order and reduce confusion. They provide clarity over who owns what and under what rights. This in turn reduces disputes and lowers the risk in transactions. If one is buying a piece of land, one wants to know the person selling it has the legal right to do so. A formal registry in charge of property rights can have an influence on the economic outcome (Dang et al., 2020) as it gives you the trust needed. This is especially important in places where informal agreements or undocumented claims have caused conflict in the past.

But just having a land registry does not mean everyone will use it. Whether people actually rely on it in practice often comes down to trust. Trust in the system. Trust in the people running it. Xie & Xu (2024) studied this in China and found a clear split. People were more likely to transfer land if they trusted the person they were dealing with. But when it came to putting that deal into a formal, written contract, what mattered more was their trust in the institution, the village authority, in that case. Without that kind of institutional trust, people stuck to informal deals or skipped the paperwork entirely.

This shows that it is not just about having a working registry. It is about whether people believe it works for them. If they think the information can be tampered with, or that disputes will not be fairly resolved, they will not feel safe using it, even if everything looks fine on paper. Teraji (2008) brings it to the point elegantly. Without trust, rights do not mean much. It is not enough to have property rights on the books; they need to be backed by a system people believe in. That belief lowers the need for constant checking, extra agreements, or backup plans. In other words, it is trust that allows the system to run smoothly in the background.

To sum up this section, land administration systems play a central role in providing clarity, legal certainty, and reducing disputes in real estate transactions. But as shown above, having a registry in place does not automatically mean that people will trust or use it the way it is intended. In practice, it often comes down to whether people believe the system works for them, and whether the institutions behind it are reliable. Trust, both interpersonal and institutional, plays a big role here. This is exactly where blockchain enters the conversation. Much has been said about blockchain's potential to increase transparency, reduce fraud, and improve trust in systems like these. But before going into whether or not blockchain can actually help fix some of these issues, it is worth taking a step back and first understanding what blockchain is and how it works.

4.2 Blockchain Fundamentals in the Context of Land Registries

In this section the main principles behind blockchain technology will be introduced, with a focus on how it works in practice and how its core ideas might be relevant in the context of land registration. Since blockchain is a term that is often used but rarely fully understood, this section aims to present its mechanics in a straightforward way, particularly for those readers without a technical background in blockchain or computer science. This section is particularly important as in order to explore its uses in land registries one should first understand the structure and behavior of blockchain. Note, however, that while this research aims to give an understanding of the technology, a full technological analysis and explanation of the detailed workings of the technology is outside the scope of this work.

Put simply, a blockchain is a digital system for recording transactions. But unlike a more traditional database, where a central authority can add, remove, or change entries at will, blockchain works more like a chain of blocks that are added one after another in a way that makes tampering quite difficult. Each new block is "chained" to the previous one using cryptographic methods, essentially complicated math that makes it practically impossible to change something without everyone noticing (Yaga et al., 2018).

Each block holds a group of transactions, like for example property transfers, and each one is stamped with a time, a digital fingerprint, and a link to the block before it. These fingerprints, called hashes, are what keep the chain secure. Even the smallest change in a block, like trying to alter the owner of a piece of land, would change its hash and alert the system that something is wrong (Yaga et al., 2018; Zheng et al., 2017). This structure makes blockchain an appealing tool for keeping trustworthy records that cannot be quietly altered later. Another major feature of blockchain is that it is typically made to be decentralized. In simpler terms, this means there is no single person or authority in control. Instead, the same copy of the blockchain exists on many different computers, sometimes thousands, spread all around the world. Every time someone wants to add a new block, it first hast to be checked by the rest of the network to make sure that its valid. If it is, everyone adds it to their copy. This collective agreement is called "consensus," and it is what ensures the blockchain is consistent and reliable without needing a central gatekeeper (Tripathi et al., 2023; Yaga et al., 2018).

Blockchain networks agree on what gets added in a variety of different ways. The most well-known method is called Proof of Work. This method involves computers competing to solve a difficult mathematical problem, and the first one to solve it gets to add the next block. While this method is secure, it also uses a huge amount of electricity, which makes it impractical for many real-world systems like land administration (Zheng et al., 2017).

So, what exactly does this mean for land registries? Due to the nature of land registries, the kind of blockchain that would be used in land administration is unlikely to be fully decentralized. Instead, it would be a so called *permissioned blockchain,* which means that only certain actors (such as government agencies or approved institutions) would be allowed to update the ledger (or database). In this case, the blockchain would still provide benefits like transparency, security, and traceability (Yaga et al., 2018), but it would not be open to everyone in the way that systems like Bitcoin or Ethereum are.

These permissioned blockchains are essentially semi-private systems. They are faster and more efficient than public blockchains because they rely on a smaller, trusted group to validate transactions. But this means that they lose the full decentralization that is often considered one of blockchain's most defining features (Zheng et al., 2017). Put in different words, the trust in the system no longer comes from the crowd, but from the assumption that the chosen validators (Administrators) are acting in good faith.

This centralization, however, is not necessarily a drawback in land administration, where records have always been managed by authorities like land registries. In fact, by using blockchain in a permissioned model, registries can retain oversight and compliance control, while also gaining the benefits of a tamper-proof record and improved data integrity (Tripathi et al., 2023). As long as the system is designed with strong rules about who can participate and how consensus is reached, it can still be a major improvement over current systems where errors or fraud can go unnoticed for years.

To sum up, blockchain is not one single thing or platform one can subscribe to. It is a structure that can be adapted to fit different purposes. When applied to land registries, it would need to be tailored as a permissioned system, meaning the decentralization would be reduced. However, the gains in transparency, auditability, and data reliability could still make it a great solution for improving public trust and administrative efficiency in land management.

4.3 State of Current Land Registry Systems

Before diving into what blockchain can do to improve LAS, it is worth getting a clear picture of the systems currently in place. This section looks at how land registries typically work today, what their pain points are, and why they are still a long way from being seamless, especially in a digital world. The goal here is to understand the system blockchain is trying to improve (or disrupt), without yet talking about blockchain itself.

4.3.1 What "normal" looks like

Most countries operate on either a deed-based or title-based land registry system. Title-based systems confirm ownership rights outright, while deed-based systems just record documents, the actual legal standing still has to be verified elsewhere. Different countries take different approaches, but the main takeaway is that these systems were not exactly built with the modern world in mind as they have already become outdated (Križanović et al., 2021).

A typical land transfer is anything but straightforward. The process involves multiple departments and actors (lawyers, agents, officials), and steps that include verifying ownership, drafting contracts, registering deeds, and updating records at revenue offices. It is not just slow it is fragmented and hard to navigate leading to differing information (Shuaib et al., 2022).

To understand where the problems lie, it is helpful to walk through what a typical land transaction looks like today, or rather, what it is supposed to look like. While the exact steps may vary slightly by country or even region, the basic flow is pretty standard. And yes, it is as tedious as it sounds.

According to Shuaib et al. (2022), the land transfer process is generally structured around "deed registration," where the deed serves as proof of the transaction but does not automatically validate ownership. The process has a lot of moving parts, and each one has to go right for the next to happen.

Here is what it usually looks like, step by step (Shuaib et al., 2022):

1. **Ownership check:** First and foremost, you need to confirm that the person selling the land is actually the one who owns it. If there are no red flags, things can move forward.
2. **Sale agreement:** A basic agreement is signed between buyer and seller, usually including a sum of money (kind of like a deposit) paid upfront.

3. **Payment of fees:** The buyer pays registration fees either online or at a local treasury office, one of several transactions still often done in person.
4. **Deed drafting:** The actual land deed is written up on official paper which has been stamped by the relevant official. Around this time, the main purchase funds are transferred from buyer to seller. The deal is then signed and witnessed.
5. **Registrar submission:** The paperwork is submitted to the local registrar's office. This is where identity verification and property mapping take place. If everything checks out, the registered deed is issued.
6. **Revenue office update:** With the deed in hand, the buyer goes to the city or state land revenue office to update the official land records.
7. **Public announcement and objections:** The revenue office records statements from both sides and issues a public notice inviting objections. If no one contests the deal, the records are updated, and the transaction is finalized.

As the authors point out, "every step contains conditions" that must be met before moving forward, which is a polite way of saying the process is slow, manual, and vulnerable to delays or manipulation at pretty much any stage.

4.3.2 Core issues with current systems

There is a long list of problems with the way land registries function today. A few that come up again and again (Janbandhu et al., 2023):

- **Everything is scattered**: Different departments hold different pieces of the puzzle, and they do not always talk to each other. This leads to duplicated work, inconsistent records, and confusion.
- **Too many people have their hands in the pot**: The process is packed with intermediaries, which adds time, cost, and fraud risk.
- **No single source of truth**: Even if one thinks one has found the right document, one often has to go digging through others to confirm it.
- **Old-fashioned storage**: Many records are still on paper, (yes, actual paper) which makes them easy to lose, destroy, or tamper with.

And even when countries make the jump to digital systems, those often do not fix much. Many "digital" platforms were just built to replicate old paper formats. They still rely on central servers, outdated structures, and poor coordination (Križanović et al., 2021).

4.3.3 Going digital is not always an upgrade

One would think that digitization would solve most of the above, but the reality is more complicated. In many places, going digital has just meant putting the same clunky paper records into a new, centralized database, same problems, new format. As R. M. Bennett et al. (2021) point out, governments often focus on building digital systems but forget about maintaining them. That means data quality is poor, outdated entries, and rules about how and when records should be updated are not at all clear. Add in the occasional cybersecurity risk (such as hacking attacks), and you end up with a system that looks modern on the surface but is still hard to trust.

4.3.4 Vulnerability to Fraud and Manipulation

One of the biggest thorns in the side of existing land administration systems is how prone they are to fraud, and not just in theory. Whether through forged documents, double registrations, or "disappearing" titles, the reality is that these systems often do not do enough to stop bad actors from gaming the process.

A big part of this has to do with the structure of most land registries today. They are centralized, meaning the control lies with a single authority or office, and that setup comes with its own risks. In many cases, this centralized control opens the door to corrupt practices or inside manipulation of land ownership records (Shuaib et al., 2022).

Janbandhu et al. (2023) add that land records are often outdated, incomplete, or simply missing. In some cases where records can be found these documents are sometimes in such a bad state that the information on them can barely be read. This creates confusion over who actually owns what, which in turn becomes fertile ground for disputes and scams.

Paper records make things worse. They are fragile, easy to alter or destroy, and often stored in conditions that do not meet basic standards of security.

Theft, fire, and deliberate tampering are not just hypothetical, they are very real threats (Janbandhu et al., 2023).

So, while digitization is often hailed as a fix, it does not automatically eliminate the risk of fraud, especially if the digital version is still controlled by the same central actors or is based on flawed, pre-existing data. In short, if the system is corruptible on paper, making it digital does not change much unless something else fundamentally shifts.

The current way land registries work is not the best and leaves room for improvements. It is slow, scattered, and vulnerable to all sorts of issues, from administrative delays to straight-up fraud. Even digital versions do not always help, since most are just rebranded versions of outdated paper processes. So, if this is the system to be dealt with, the natural next question becomes: what could actually fix it? That is where blockchain comes in. The next section explores the theory behind using blockchain in land registration, and why, at least on paper, it sounds like the perfect match.

4.4 Blockchain in Land Registries: Possibilities and Challenges

Speak to anyone in the industry, and you'll likely hear a consistent refrain: land registries are notoriously slow, overly complex, and burdened with outdated processes. Paper trails, bureaucracy, and in some parts of the world corruption, are unfortunately not uncommon. It is no wonder then that blockchain (BC) has been looked at as a way to bring real change to the land admin space. But while there has been a lot of excitement around what blockchain could do, there is a very different conversation when you look at what has in fact happened when people tried to implement it.

This section is about that gap. First, the main theoretical benefits that blockchain is said to bring to land registries will be presented. Then, an analysis of the problems that have come up when those ideas met real-world systems, laws, and institutions will be carried out.

4.4.1 What Blockchain Could Do

One of the most widely shared ideas is that blockchain offers immutability. Meaning once something gets recorded, it is locked in and cannot be tampered. In a land registry context, this would mean no one can just "change" ownership records or tamper with the title without leaving a visible trace (Kaczorowska, 2019). This is particularly important in places where land fraud is a real issue.

On top of that, blockchain brings transparency. With the right access rules, anyone involved in a land transaction could independently verify title status or track the chain of ownership, without having to go through a slow, centralized registry office (Mezquita et al., 2021). That level of openness could cut down corruption and boost public trust.

Then there is the speed and cost argument. Transactions that currently take weeks or even months to process, because of intermediaries like lawyers, notaries, and paper forms, could be reduced to a few days or hours. This could be made possible using smart contracts, pieces of code that trigger actions like ownership transfers when certain conditions are met (Daniel & Ifejika Speranza, 2020).

Some researchers also point to the economic potential of secure land rights. If people have guaranteed, transparent ownership titles, they are more likely to use land as collateral for loans or invest in it. This, in theory, could support local development and open up property markets (Mansoor et al., 2023).

And now to the big one: decentralization. A lot of the hype around blockchain comes from the fact that it does not need a central authority. But that is where land administration gets a bit tricky. Property law is almost always tied to state institutions. Land titles, after all, are legally recognized because the government says they are.

So full decentralization, where no central body is in charge, is not actually a good fit for this space. That does not mean blockchain is useless here, it just means the version that works best is probably a private or hybrid one, where the core land authority still exists, but uses blockchain to record and manage data securely (Thomas, 2017).

4.4.2 What Gets in the Way

Of course, all of the above sounds great, on paper. But once things move beyond theory, serious issues start to appear.

First, there is the legal problem. Land ownership is defined and protected by law. One cannot just record something on a blockchain and expect it to be legally binding unless the legal system says it is. Right now, most property laws around the world are not set up to recognize blockchain entries as official proof of ownership (Thomas, 2017). He goes as far as calling it "nonsensical to consider that an online code is in any way definitive of legal rights" (Thomas, 2017).

Then there is scalability and integration. Land registries do not operate in a vacuum. They are connected to courts, banks, tax systems, and planning departments. If a blockchain solution does not integrate with all of these, it will not be much use. In fact, many pilot projects fail exactly because they were built in isolation and could not "talk" to the rest of the system (Tan et al., 2022).

Institutional resistance is another big one. Changing how land registries work means changing how people work, and not everyone is on board with that. Staff might feel threatened, especially if the new system removes their discretionary power or makes their job redundant. In some cases, entire departments have quietly resisted or blocked pilot projects out of fear of losing control (Mansoor et al., 2023).

Another point worth mentioning is that decentralization brings its own risks. For example, if you let just anyone write to the chain, how do you make sure transaction order is accurate? What if two people try to register ownership of the same plot at nearly the same time? Traditional registries solve this with timestamping and control. A blockchain without that kind of governance could end up creating more confusion than clarity (Kaczorowska, 2019).

Accountability is another unresolved issue. In most countries, if something goes wrong in the land registry, the government can be held responsible. But if the system is run on a decentralized ledger, who is liable if a title is wrong? Who do you sue? Who fixes it? Without clear answers, blockchain could actually weaken institutional accountability rather than strengthen it (Thomas, 2017).

And finally, education. Possibly the most underestimated barrier. Saari et al. (2022) make this point clear: without a solid base of digital literacy, blockchain projects are unlikely to take off. Registry officials, legal professionals, and even private-sector actors often do not have the technical know-how to adopt or manage these systems. On top of that, the public has to trust and use the system too, which will not happen if they do not understand how it works. Education is not a "nice-to-have" it is central. The authors point to the need for targeted training programs, integration into higher education, and long-term skill-building across both the public and private sectors.

They also flag related concerns: lack of common standards, cybersecurity vulnerabilities (especially around interfaces and external data sources), and the fact that many property records are still only partially digitized, if at all. If the base data is not reliable, putting it on blockchain does not help. It just makes bad data harder to fix.

There is clearly no shortage of theoretical benefits when it comes to using blockchain in land registries. Immutability, transparency, cost savings, and the possibility of automating trust all sound good. But once you leave the whiteboard and enter the real world, things get messy. Legal uncertainty, integration issues, institutional pushback, data quality concerns, and plain old human resistance are just some of the roadblocks. And as Saari et al. (2022) show, none of this will work unless people are properly trained, not just to use the systems, but to believe in them.

That does not mean blockchain has no place here. It just means the conversation needs to move past buzzwords and into the details. The next section will dive into real-life case studies to see what has actually happened when blockchain was introduced to land registries, and what lessons we can take from those experiences.

4.5 Overview of Past Projects and Case Studies

By now, it is clear that blockchain has made its way into just about every industry slide deck and innovation lab, but what about actual, on-the-ground land registries? A lot has been said about how blockchain could fix land administration. However, what happens when you try to do it? This section looks at four key case studies, Sweden, Georgia, Ghana, and India (Andhra Pradesh), where blockchain was not just theorized but tested or deployed. Each example gives us something to work with. While none of them led to full-scale national adoption, they help us start answering the central question of this research: what works, what does not, and why?

Before getting into each case study, it is worth noting that these will be the case studies analyzed in the main research part of this paper. The specific guidelines for choosing each paper are further elaborated in the methodology section however the overall choice of case studies was primarily guided by the availability and quantity of literature. With this in mind, it should be stated that the case of Georgia was the one with the least availability literature even though it is one of the ones that went the furthest. There were considerations of removing Georgia as a potential case study to be analyzed. However, due to its success, an effort was still made to keep it inside this paper.

4.5.1 Sweden

The Swedish case study was one of the first and most cited attempts to use blockchain in land administration. The project was driven by Lantmäteriet (Sweden's land registry authority) in collaboration with ChromaWay, Telia, Kairos Future, and a few banks (McMurren et al., 2018; *The Land Registry in the Blockchain*, 2016). The goal of this pilot project was rather straightforward: reduce the time and paperwork involved in buying and registering property. For that, they used ChromaWay's Postchain, a permissioned (consortium-style blockchain), and Esplix, a smart contract platform, to automate workflows (McMurren et al., 2018; Rodima-Taylor, 2021). It was never scaled and rolled out to the public, but the proof-of-concept worked well and was estimated to save over €100 million per year in admin costs if implemented nationwide (Rodima-Taylor, 2021).

4.5.2 Georgia

Georgia went about it differently, and arguably, more effectively. Instead of building something new from scratch, they simply added a blockchain layer on top of their already existing digital land registry. The whole thing was rolled out in collaboration with Bitfury and was later backed by the Blockchain Trust Accelerator and economist Hernando de Soto (Shang & Price, 2019). On the technical side, they used Exonum, Bitfury's own permissioned blockchain framework, which they then anchored to the Bitcoin blockchain. The idea was to store hashes of land records using Merkle Trees, which made it possible to verify the integrity of documents publicly without exposing any private data (Shang & Price, 2019). And this was not just another pilot, by 2018, more than 1.5 million titles had been hashed to Bitcoin. This one actually went live and ran (Shang & Price, 2019). Which will be an interesting case study to analyze as undoubtedly, they will have faced problems and finding out how they resolved them could be of particular value.

4.5.3 Ghana

Ghana's efforts were less centralized and came from different directions. One initiative came from a startup called BenBen, which built a private blockchain platform to digitize land records and help connect buyers, banks, and the Lands Commission (Ameyaw, 2024). Another came from Bitland Global, which launched a public blockchain pilot in Kumasi to help local communities register land themselves (Rodima-Taylor, 2021). Unlike Georgia or Sweden, Ghana experimented with both private and public blockchains. BenBen focused on institutional coordination. Bitland focused more on community access. Both showed promise but have remained limited to pilot stages and small-scale usage.

4.5.4 India (Andhra Pradesh)

In India, the most notable example comes from the state of Andhra Pradesh and its capital city, Amaravati. The Capital Region Development Authority (CRDA) ran a project that aimed to manage land pooling and registration using blockchain (Kshetri, 2022). Here, too, the blockchain was permissioned, set up in collaboration with ChromaWay, local tech firm Zebi, and advisory support from ConsenSys (Bhattacharya, 2018; Kshetri, 2022).

The system registered over 100,000 plots using GPS data, Aadhaar numbers, and QR-coded digital titles. Over 24,000 farmers participated, exchanging their land for serviced plots in the new city (Bhattacharya, 2018). Registrations that used to take weeks were done in hours.

4.5.5 Common Pitfalls

So, what held these projects back? A few common themes showed up across the board. First was the legal side; blockchain data was not always recognized in court or by law, which made it risky to rely on it fully. This was a problem in both Sweden (McMurren et al., 2018). Second, there was the trust issue. In India and Ghana, people were skeptical that blockchain would fix anything if the institutions behind it were still the same (Bhattacharya, 2018; Rodima-Taylor, 2021). Then came the tech literacy gap. Especially in places where many had little or no experience with digital systems, blockchain was too abstract to build user confidence (Ameyaw & de Vries, 2023). And lastly, even when the technology worked, projects often failed to grow. A lack of political will, regulation, or inter-agency coordination meant that many stayed stuck in the early phases (Kshetri, 2022).

In other words, blockchain has been tried, and it has shown some real potential. But there is still a long way from any kind of widespread or permanent adoption. The examples above help illustrate what can go right. But maybe more importantly, they also show us what tends to go wrong. And so, the obvious next question becomes: What are the actual barriers? What keeps blockchain from making it all the way through?

All things considered, blockchain does seem like a natural fit to solve many of the issues currently faced by land registries. The theory promises a lot, immutability, transparency, faster processing times, and reduced reliance on middlemen. And to be fair, some of the projects reviewed have shown that these benefits are technically possible. But if something is "technically possible" that is still very different from being "widely adopted". From legal gaps and integration issues to lack of training and institutional pushback, there is a long list of reasons why the adoption of blockchain has not taken off at scale. The case studies discussed above show both the potential and the friction. So now that the key concepts have been laid out and real-world trials explored, the next section will explain how this research aims to dig deeper. Specifically, the methodology will cover how the case studies were selected, how the analysis will be carried out, and what the research hopes to uncover when it comes to blockchain's practical use in land registries.

5 Methodology

5

This thesis takes a qualitative, cross-case approach to understanding the recurring roadblocks in blockchain implementation for land registries across a series of selected real-world case studies. The general goal is not to confirm a theory but to map out recurring patterns across multiple contexts. This method follows the comparative logic laid out by Miles et al. (2014) who argue that well-designed cross-case analysis helps both in surfacing robust insights and increasing the applicability of findings to other similar contexts.

In other words, the goal in not just asking "what went wrong here?", but rather, "what tends to go wrong again and again?" This section will go over how the cases were picked, how the data was collected and analyzed, and what steps were taken to make sure that the findings are reliable and grounded in evidence.

Some critics of the technique argue that aiming for generalizability is not appropriate in qualitative research. Miles, Huberman, and Saldaña, however, directly address this concern:

> *"One reason to conduct a cross-case analysis is to enhance generalizability or transferability to other contexts. Although it's argued that this goal is sometimes inappropriate for qualitative studies, the question does not go away. We would like to know something about the relevance or applicability of our findings to other similar settings, to transcend the particular in order to understand the general. Just adding cases is a brute-force approach that will not help. But multiple cases, adequately sampled (Are they typical? Are they diverse? Are they unusually effective or ineffective?) and analyzed carefully can help us answer the reasonable question: Do these findings apply beyond this one specific case?" (Miles et al., 2014)*

P. L. Reiser et al., *Blockchain in Global Land Registries*,
https://doi.org/10.1007/978-3-658-50076-4_5

Their point is clear: if done thoughtfully, with well-chosen and diverse cases, cross-case analysis can help us move beyond individual case conclusions without falling into the trap of oversimplification.

This approach is designed to systematically compare multiple real-world cases to identify patterns, recurring challenges, and explanatory insights. It is often used to compare and contrast multiple real-life case studies to see what patterns emerge. In the particular situation of this research, instead of focusing on just one pilot project and drawing conclusions from that, it will look across several and try to identify recurring themes or roadblocks that may be getting in the way of implementation.

The methodology comprises three key sections as follows:

1. Case selection and sampling
2. Data collection workflow
3. Coding and cross case analysis

5.1 Case Selection and Sampling

Because this research relies heavily on the selected cases to draw its conclusions, the first step is also the most important. Namely, that of selecting which cases will make it into the research, and for each case which information.

In this context, each case is a specific blockchain pilot or implementation attempt in land registry or land administration which have been tried in different countries. To choose them, a purposive sampling method will be used, which means cases that were information-rich and relevant for the research question were deliberately chosen, a strategy endorsed by Miles et al., for multiple-case designs (Miles et al., 2014, pp. 31–32) .

Each case had to meet the following basic conditions:

- The project involves a real-world attempt to implement or ascertain the feasibility of implementing blockchain in land registration or administration.
- Sufficient and credible documentation of the case exists (specific types mentioned below).

- The case has to offer rich detail: enough so that not just what happened, but what went wrong or what was challenging could be understood.
- The cases must represent a range of geographical locations to allow cross jurisdictional trend analysis and add a further layer of robustness to the research, by not focusing solely on one location.

Once each case study is found, a second round of sampling will be done where the actual data sources for each of the selected cases will be gathered. In terms of content the documents to be included must at least mention the relevant case study and speak about challenges in implementing blockchain into the land administration / registry systems. In order to maintain the integrity and validity of the findings the documents and sources for each case must meet at least one of the types listed below:

- Official government documents and press releases
- Academic articles (incl. Journal articles, approved preprints, Thesis)
- Industry reports or whitepapers (incl. Conference Papers)
- Stakeholder interviews
- Credible news or interview features
- Reports by international organizations (e.g. UN, World Bank)

5.2 Data Collection Workflow

Documents and sources will be sourced primarily using Google Scholar for academic publications. To locate non-academic materials, such as news articles, press releases, and reports, tools like Google Search and AI-powered engines (such as Perplexity and ChatGPT-4o) will be used. Perplexity is preferred over ChatGPT for its superior focus on sourcing and data transparency, which supports citation tracking. However, ChatGPT will still be used in order to find any other documents and sources that may be of interest to the research.

All gathered documents will be saved in Zotero for reference management in order to align with the overall reference management for the whole thesis. The documents will also be imported into MAXQDA24 Analytics Pro, which will be used for the qualitative coding and cross-case comparison.

5.3 Coding and Cross-Case Analysis

Once all the data sources have been compiled into MAXQDA24, the data analysis will begin. This will also be done in line with concepts described by Miles et al. (2014) and Saldaña (2021). Each source will be analyzed and coded in a case-by-case basis before moving on to a cross case comparison of the existence of different codes across cases. Coding will be carried out in a three-step approach involving two cycles of codes and one Thematic result:

1. **First Cycle – Descriptive Coding:** Here, segments of text are labelled with what they are about in general. For example, if a report says, "data transparency was a problem," it gets tagged accordingly. This is done in order to summarize the basic ideas or topics from a passage into a single word or a phrase (Miles et al., 2014, p. 74) Here it is important to note that the descriptive codes should not be a summary of the content but rather an identification of the topic which is being discussed (Saldaña, 2021).

   Further remarks in relation to the first cycle codes:

   1. "Descriptive codes" was chosen for this stage as this type is well suited for the type of data that will be analyzed: documents, journals, and other texts (Saldaña, 2021)
   2. The codes will be done inductively. As Saldaña (2021) puts it, this way enters the analysis with an open mind and "spontaneously creates original codes the first time data are reviewed."
   3. Having said this, once the first few sources have been coded, if data is found in subsequent sources that can be described with codes already made previously, the existing codes will be used. This would closer resemble what Saldaña (2021) describes as deductive coding even if the list of codes was not prepared before analysis or "prior to field work."

2. **Second Cycle – Pattern Coding:** The second cycle of coding is the step wherein the material from the first cycle are ordered into "a smaller number of categories, themes, or constructs" (Miles et al., 2014). This cycle aims to infer from the first cycle codes underlying themes by pulling "together a lot of material from first cycle coding into more meaningful and parsimonious units of analysis" (Saldaña, 2021). So, for example "data

transparency" might link to a broader concern about governance or legacy IT systems.

3. **Pattern/Themes Matrix:** The final themes which emerge from the Second cycle are distilled from the interpretive layer and will later e displayed in the cross-case comparison tables and Matrix Displays (Miles et al., 2014). This is the table where the presence of different themes will be shown across cases and whereupon conclusions will be drawn.

Once the main themes have been identified through coding, the first step will be to lay them out in a factor evidence table. This table will list each roadblock (or theme) along with a direct quote from the source material that shows exactly where it was mentioned (Appendix 2). The idea here is to make things as transparent as possible, so that every interpretation in the analysis can be traced directly back to the original text. No guesswork, just evidence.

After that, the data will be summarized into a Summed Indices Matrix (Table 2) based on the method outlined by (Miles & Huberman, 1994). This is essentially a table where each row is one of the identified themes and each column is one of the case studies. If a theme was clearly present in a case, it gets marked with a «✓». This format makes it easy to spot patterns: which issues showed up again and again, and which ones were specific to certain contexts or jurisdictions.

6 Data / Information Source

To gather the information needed for this research, a mix of different search tools was used, all of which helped to find the specific types of sources mentioned in the methodology section. Most of the material came from online searches, including Google Scholar, Google, Perplexity, and ChatGPT.

Each tool served a slightly different purpose. Google Scholar was mainly used to find academic sources: journal articles, theses, and other peer-reviewed content. For industry reports, government press releases, or official documents, regular Google searches proved most useful. Perplexity was helpful to get a quick overview of publicly available information or locate harder-to-find sources, especially those not indexed in academic databases. Lastly, ChatGPT was used more as a research assistant, to brainstorm case leads, generate search terms, and help refine queries. Of course, anything found this way was cross-checked through more conventional sources before being included.

Search terms were adapted depending on what was being looked for and where. For example, to find information on blockchain pilots in land registries, phrases such as *"blockchain land registry pilot [country name]"* or *"DLT in land administration [country] challenges"* were used in Google Scholar. In the case of using Perplexity and ChatGPT prompts such as the following were used to find data sources for the research (Figure 1).

The prompt was then adapted by changing the name of the country in order to find information on all case studies. Additionally, the prompt above was adapted by naming less source types so it could focus on finding specific document types. In those cases, prompts such as the following were used (Figure 2).

P. L. Reiser et al., *Blockchain in Global Land Registries*,
https://doi.org/10.1007/978-3-658-50076-4_6

"You are tasked with finding credible and detailed information about *challenges*, encountered during pilot projects to implement blockchain into the land registry system in Sweden. Focus exclusively on trusted and verifiable sources, including: Official Swedish government reports or press releases, academic sources (peer-reviewed journal articles, university theses, or approved preprints), industry whitepapers or conference presentations from relevant stakeholders, Interviews or public statements from involved stakeholders, credible mainstream or specialized news features covering the pilot, reports or commentary from international organizations (e.g. World Bank, UN, OECD). Only include sources that explicitly discuss obstacles, failures, or implementation difficulties, not just benefits or general overviews. Provide citation details (title, author, date, source link)."

Figure 1: **Example prompt used for research with GenAI**

"Your task is to identify academic literature that discusses challenges, problems, or limitations encountered during the pilot project to implement blockchain technology in Sweden's land registry system. Limit your search strictly to scholarly and academic sources, including Peer-reviewed journal articles, University-level master's or doctoral theses, Approved preprints from reputable platforms (e.g. SSRN, institutional repositories). Focus only on documents that explicitly address implementation difficulties, such as legal, technical, organizational, or user adoption challenges, rather than general overviews or theoretical benefits. For each relevant document, summarize the key points regarding the encountered problems and provide full citation details (title, author(s), publication year, type of document, and link or DOI if available)."

Figure 2: **Example prompt used for further research with GenAI**

The goal throughout was not just to gather as much of material as possible, but to find information that actually met the inclusion criteria, meaning sources that were detailed, relevant, credible, and had mentions of barriers or problems. Out of around 150 sources that initially seemed to match the search terms, only about 30 ended up being useful for the research. The main reason for this drop was that many of the earlier picks did not mention any specific challenges encountered in the projects, which, as outlined in the methodology, was a key requirement. This alone was one of the biggest reasons the list shrank so much. Still, using a mix of different platforms allowed for a broader and more flexible search strategy, which helped ensure that each case was backed by reliable data and came with perspectives from different angles.

The following table compiles the final 30 sources that were used in the analysis stage. The table is ordered by which case study the source it is relevant for, including its title, what type of source it is and the corresponding reference.

Table 1: **Sources used in analysis**

Case	Title	Type	Source
Sweden	Hybrid Approaches for Smart Contracts in Land Administration: Lessons from Three Blockchain Proofs-of-Concept	Journal Article	R. Bennett et al., 2021
Sweden	Blockchain Adoption is an Evolution – not a Revolution: Advantages and Challenges of Blockchain in Real Estate Transaction in Sweden	Thesis	Djursén & Björk, 2022
Sweden	Legal challenges and opportunities of blockchain technology in the real estate sector	Journal Article	Garcia-Teruel, 2020
Sweden	Sweden Moves to Next Stage with Blockchain Land Registry	News Article	Jonathan, 2021
Sweden	Perceived Affordance and Socio-Technical Transition: Blockchain for the Swedish Public Sector	Thesis	Jonsson, 2018
Sweden	Balancing Blockchain and AI: ChromaWay and the Swedish Land Registry Submit Findings for Government Report	Interview	Jorgen, 2021
Sweden	Addressing Transaction Costs Through Blockchain and Identity in Swedish Land Transfers	Industry / Government Report	McMurren et al., 2018
Sweden	Blockchain, a Feasible Technology for Land Administration?	Conference Paper	Müller & Seifert, 2019
Sweden	The blockchain challenge for Sweden's housing and mortgage markets	Journal Article	Proskurovska & Dörry, 2022
Sweden	Current Status, Requirements, and Challenges of Blockchain Application in Land Registry	Journal Article	Shuaib et al., 2022
Georgia	A systematic review of the institutional success factors for blockchain-based land administration	Journal Article	Ansah et al., 2023

Case	Title	Type	Source
Georgia	Anti-corruption reforms have been successful in Georgia, but blockchain is stealing the limelight	News Publication	Aarvik, 2024
Georgia	Land registries on a distributed ledger	Institutional Report	v. Weizsäcker et al., 2018
Georgia	Integration of Blockchain Technology into a Land Registration System for Immutable Traceability: A Casestudy of Georgia	Conference Paper	Lazuashvili et al., 2019
Georgia	A Blockchain-Based Land Titling Project in the Republic of Georgia: Rebuilding Public Trust and Lessons for Future Pilot Projects	Journal Article	Shang & Price, 2019
Ghana	Blockchain Technology for a Transparent Land Administration System: Feasibility Assessment for Adoption in Ghana's Land Sector	Thesis	Ameyaw, 2024
Ghana	Toward Smart Land Management: Land Acquisition and the Associated Challenges in Ghana. A Look into a Blockchain Digital Land Registry for Prospects	Journal Article	Ameyaw & de Vries, 2021
Ghana	Blockchain technology adaptation for land administration services: The importance of socio-cultural elements	Journal Article	Ameyaw & de Vries, 2023
Ghana	Barriers to the Adoption of Blockchain for Land Administration in a Developing Economy	Conference Paper	Baako et al., 2022
Ghana	Bitland Blockchain Initiative Seeks to Create Reliable Land Titles In Africa	News Article	Coleman, 2016
Ghana	Beyond the Hype: Exploring Blockchain Technology in Land Administration	Thesis	Olsen, 2018
Ghana	Blockchain Technology in Lands Registration: A Systematic Literature Review	Journal Article	Zein & Twinomurinzi, 2023
India	Blockchain is helping build a new Indian city, but it's no cure for corruption	News Article	Bhattacharya, 2018
India	Can Blockchain Solve Corruption Problems in Land Administration in Developing Countries? – The Case of India	Thesis	Comincioli, 2021
India	Land Record Management in India	Preprint	Kapoor et al., 2024
India	New technology interventions including blockchain technology in land record and registry management in India	Conference Paper	Kaushik, 2020
India	Blockchain as a tool to facilitate property rights protection in the Global South: lessons from India's Andhra Pradesh state	Journal Article	Kshetri, 2022

■ Data / Information Source

Case	Title	Type	Source
India	The Applicability of Blockchain Technology in Land Registration for Developing Economies: A Case Study of India	Preprint	Kumar & Motwani, 2025
India	Blockchain and Government	Article in Book	A. Sharma et al., 2021
India	Analysis of the barriers of blockchain adoption in Land Record System	Article in Book	P. Sharma et al., 2022

7 Analysis

Before diving into the core findings, it's useful to take a first look at the two charts below. These provide a visual overview of how often each barrier was identified across the case studies. While they offer some interesting takeaways at a glance, it's important to note that these charts are included purely for visualisation purposes and should not be treated as quantitative evidence in and of themselves.

7

The primary focus of this research is not to count how many times a problem was mentioned, but to examine the nature and context of the barriers that emerged in each case. The number of mentions per barrier is heavily influenced by the quantity and depth of the available literature per country, which varies significantly. Drawing any conclusions based purely on frequency would therefore risk misrepresenting the severity or importance of a given issue.

Nevertheless, these visualisations still serve a useful purpose. They help map the terrain by offering a high-level view of which barriers were most commonly brought up, and in which case studies they tended to appear. This allows for a smoother transition into the more detailed, qualitative cross-case analysis that follows, where each theme will be unpacked with close attention to how and why it arose in the respective contexts.

7.1 Data Visualization

Figure 3 shows how many times each barrier (or theme) was identified in the reviewed texts. The *Legal and Regulatory Framework* stands out as the most frequently mentioned barrier. As seen in Figure 4, this was especially the

P. L. Reiser et al., *Blockchain in Global Land Registries*,
https://doi.org/10.1007/978-3-658-50076-4_7

case in the Swedish example, where much of the discussion centered around legal concerns, particularly the status and recognition of digital signatures. This will be unpacked further in the analysis.

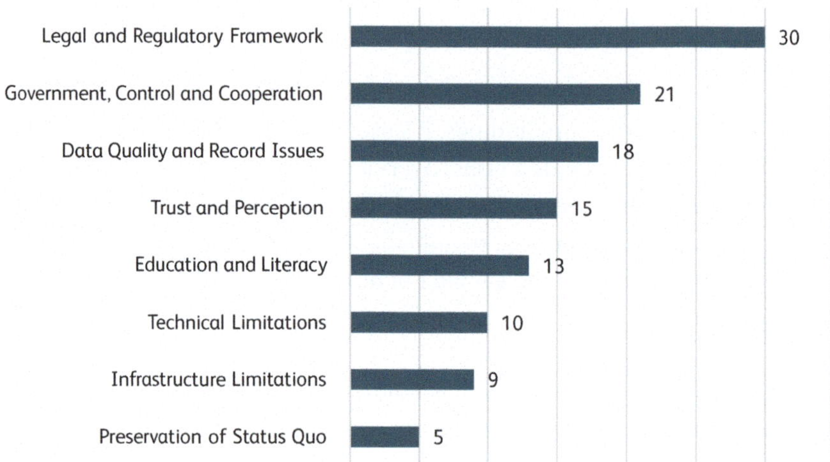

Figure 3: **Total occurrence per barrier**

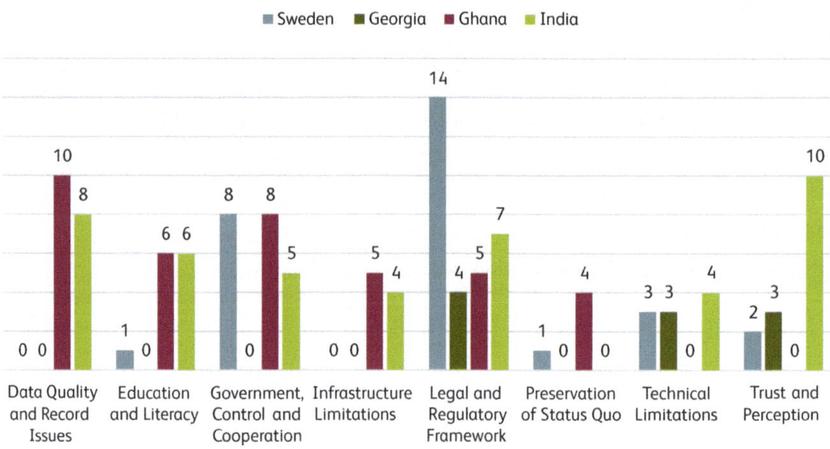

Figure 4: **Occurrence of barriers per country**

Another pattern that starts to stand out is the relatively low number of barrier mentions in the Georgian case. One possible reason for this could be that Georgia is the only case in the sample where the project is considered by some sources to have moved beyond the pilot phase and into continued use. This will be explored more closely when looking at the success factors that helped Georgia stand apart.

On the topic of success factors, it's worth clarifying why the total number of observations (the coded text segments shown in Appendix 2) doesn't exactly match the sum of the barrier mentions shown in the chart. In the case of Georgia, some of the text segments highlighted during coding described positive conditions, essentially the opposite of the barriers found in other cases. These were labelled as "*Success Factors*" rather than barriers and were therefore excluded from the chart to avoid skewing the data. In total, seven such passages were identified for Georgia, and these will be discussed in more detail in the following sections.

The patterns noted earlier are also reflected in Figure 5, which displays all the thematic barriers identified in each case study, ordered from most to least frequently observed. The higher a theme appears in each list, the more often it was flagged in the reviewed texts as a problem for blockchain implementation in that particular country.

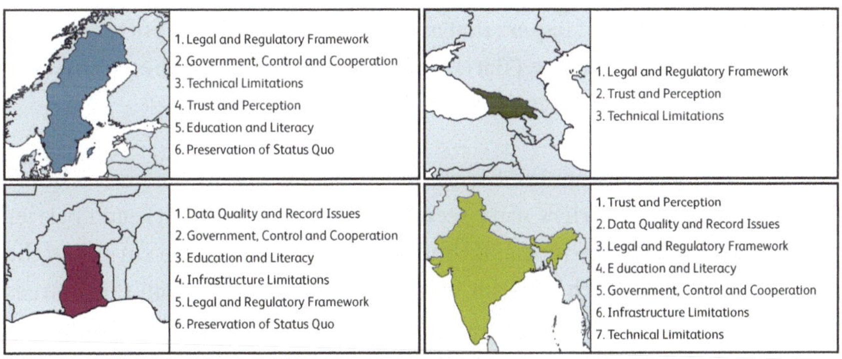

Figure 5: **Distribution of observed barriers per country**

A few surface-level observations are worth mentioning. For instance, *Data Quality and Record Issues* ranked as the most prominent barrier in Ghana and the second most in India, while it did not appear at all in the Swedish and Georgian cases. Conversely, *Legal and Regulatory Frameworks* were especially prominent in Sweden and Georgia but appeared less frequently in Ghana and India. This contrast may loosely reflect differences in institutional maturity or regulatory complexity between more and less developed economies, although this would require further investigation before any definitive claims can be made.

India presents a particularly broad spread of barriers, with seven distinct themes recorded. This may reflect the complexity of implementing blockchain across a vast and administratively diverse system, where issues range from perception and trust to infrastructure and education.

While no conclusions are drawn at this stage, this snapshot helps illustrate how certain challenges tend to cluster within specific contexts. It also sets the stage for the detailed cross-case analysis to follow, where each theme will be explored in more depth and with closer reference to the material.

7.2 Cross Case Analysis

Now that the data has been introduced and an overall perspective is formed, it is time to look at the cross-case analysis. Again, the importance of the data is not how many times it was encountered as this number would be influenced by the number of papers that are read per case. The important aspect is whether or not the theme (Barrier) was observed, or in other words, if it was mentioned in the literature or not.

The first step is to present the barrier matrix (Table 2), which gives a quick overview of which barriers were seen in each case. After that, each barrier gets its own section. The format is the same throughout: first, a cut-out of the matrix to show where the barrier was found, then quotes from the sources that show it in action. Each quote is sorted by case and color-coded to keep things clear and aid readability. At the end of the cross-case analysis section, a short separate analysis for success factors is carried out, which were seen in the case of Georgia.

Table 2: **Theme matrix showing barrier occurrence per case**

Barriers	Sweden	Georgia	Ghana	India
Legal and Regulatory Framework	✓	✓	✓	✓
Government, Control and Cooperation	✓		✓	✓
Data Quality and Record Issues			✓	✓
Trust and Perception	✓	✓		✓
Education and Literacy	✓		✓	✓
Technical Limitations	✓	✓		✓
Infrastructure Limitations			✓	✓
Preservation of Status Quo	✓		✓	

Table 3: **Barrier Abbreviations**

Barrier	Abbreviation
Legal and Regulatory Framework	LARF
Government, Control and Cooperation	GCAC
Data Quality and Record Issues	DQARI
Trust and Perception	TAP
Education and Literacy	EAL
Technical Limitations	TL
Infrastructure Limitations	IL
Preservation of Status Quo	POSQ

Overall, the most consistently observed barrier, that came up in every case study was LARF. This is evidence towards the existence of common roadblocks throughout case studies which can be used to answer RQ2 of this research, which sought to know if barriers were localized or could be encountered across jurisdictions. Along these same lines, it is interesting to note that no barrier was encountered only by one country, they were all at least found in two.

In the next part, each barrier will be shown using direct quotes from the texts where it was observed. All quotes are taken from the full list in Appendix 2.

To avoid repeating everything, only the relevant text and its reference are shown here. For the full coding and context, see Appendix 2.

7.2.1 Legal and Regulatory Framework

Table 4: **Barrier occurrence matrix (LARF)**

Sweden	Georgia	Ghana	India
✓	✓	✓	✓

Table 5: **Examples of "Legal and Regulatory Framework" in Sweden**

SE	R. Bennett et al., 2021	In terms of current status, the blockchain network and smart contract proof-of-concept protocol were trialled and externally tested. Further progress can start once the digital signature restrictions are addressed.
SE	Djursén & Björk, 2022	The second concern was the legal recognition of blockchain based contracts, with the relevant contracts still needing to be put into an EU standard format before being examined independently.
SE	Jonathan, 2021	"We want to work fully digitally, but the law requires, at the moment, physical signatures on the papers, which makes it difficult," explained Kempe.

In the case of Sweden the biggest barrier was the fact that digital signatures are not yet legally recognized, which prevents the system from working "fully digitally" (Jonathan, 2021). This is also emphasized by R. M. Bennett et al. (2021) which in their writing say that digital signatures are the one thing hindering progress in implementing blockchain into the Swedish land registry. It sounds as though the rest of the technology and systems are ready to be implemented but could not be due to the legal status of digital signatures and requirements of paper signatures. Additionally blockchain based contracts do not yet enjoy the same legal validity as conventional contracts which is mentioned by Djursén & Björk (2022) as a concern which should be addressed.

Table 6: **Examples of "Legal and Regulatory Framework" in Georgia**

GE	v. Weizsäcker et al., 2018	Secondly, the legal status of smart contracts still needs to be specified, possibly requiring 4 legal amendments of contract law, along with the changing role of the institution of the land registry. In addition, questions regarding data sovereignty are likely to arise, particularly with regards to varying privacy and data-hosting laws across different countries. Data privacy concerns may be addressed by employing cryptographic methods such as zeroknowledge proofs.
GE	Lazuashvili et al., 2019)	In the case of the Georgian government, one of the respondents admits that after the completion of the pilot project of the land titling "blockchainisation", NAPR sees the need for conducting research about the legislative framework of Georgia for supporting the further development of this blockchain project.

In Georgia further improvements are needed to the LARF in order to support the "further development of this blockchain project" (Lazuashvili et al., 2019). According to v. Weizsäcker et al. (2018) some of these improvements should be done specifically to smart contracts and their legal status which could require up to 4 amendments to the contract law, though the paper does not specify which exact amendments need to be done. So, this barrier of legal validity of smart contracts or blockchain based contracts is not just specific to Sweden but was also experienced in Georgia.

Table 7: **Examples of "Legal and Regulatory Framework" in Ghana**

GH	Baako et al., 2022	Indeed, the new Land Act, 2020 (Act 1036) makes provision for conveyancing by legal practitioners of land interests via an electronic information system; however, increased emphasis is still placed on paper-based transactions.
GH	Baako et al., 2022	Respondents were of the view that the success or otherwise of Blockchain technology, even if adopted, depended largely on the pace of justice delivery amidst an ever-increasing backlog of land disputes and litigations.

In Ghana an interesting situation was observed where even if the law provided for the use of electronic information systems for the conveyance of land interests, paper based solutions was still preferred (Baako et al., 2022). This highlights the rift between what the law as its written and what is practiced: just because the law supports a modernization, this does not mean that practitioners will be inclined to modernize.

Another problem that was faced in Ghana was the fact that there was such a "backlog of land disputes and litigations" (Baako et al., 2022) that blockchain implementation would largely depend on how quickly these could be solved. If a blockchain system is to be created each title or deed needs to be registered properly as the very nature of blockchain makes it very hard to change the records ones they have been entered into the system. If there are properties were ownership or other disputes are still being litigated no record of it can be created on the new system. These need to be resolved first.

Table 8: **Examples of "Legal and Regulatory Framework" in India**

IN	Comincioli, 2021	There are still problems deriving from the legislative systems, India and other countries have laws that prohibit the use of digital signatures or that do not take them into consideration for official documents
IN	Kshetri, 2022	The lack of blockchain standards and legal and regulatory frameworks for smart contracts has also been of concern. In smart contracts, computerised protocols and user interfaces are used to execute a contract's terms and to 'formalize and secure relationships over public networks'. AP's blockchain system uses smart contracts to allow instant data exchange with banks and financial institutions. This feature makes it possible for landowners to access loan and financial services efficiently. However, there are no clear regulations regarding smart contracts in India.

As for India, similar problems such as Sweden and Georgia were also encountered as "India and other countries have laws that prohibit the use of digital signatures" (Comincioli, 2021) which as previously mentioned for Sweden, is a cornerstone problem to the implementation of blockchain in land registries. Additionally, smart contracts also suffer from a lack in "standards and legal and regulatory frameworks" (Kshetri, 2022) as there is no real clarity for their regulation.

To sum up this section about the "Legal and Regulatory Framework" barriers, while the technology blockchain-based land registries may show promising results in proofs of concept pilot projects, legal and institutional frameworks remain significant roadblocks. Particularly the lack of recognition for digital signatures and the ambiguous status of smart contracts. Whether it is Sweden's paper signature requirements, Georgia's need for legislative amendments, Ghana's gap between law and practice, or India's lack of clarity around regulation, there seems to be a discernable theme: legal validity is a shared bottleneck. With these legal issues in mind, we now turn to explore how governments, levels of control, and forms of cooperation shape the landscape for blockchain implementation in land governance.

7.2.2 Government, Control and Cooperation

Table 9: **Barrier Occurrence Matrix (GCAC)**

Sweden	Georgia	Ghana	India
✓		✓	✓

Table 10: **Examples of "Government, Control and Cooperation" in Sweden**

SE	Proskurovska & Dörry, 2022	Interviewees Proskurovska and Dörry suggested that Lantmäteriet – currently the sole authority of Sweden's land registries – would need to cede control, but 'then the banks would also become a part of [the system] (...) And to do that we have to change the way we work together'.
SE	McMurren et al., 2018	Frameworks for data governance and the incorporation of these parties must still be defined. Thus, scalability remains a challenge.

The problem of control and cooperation between government institutions the public and other stakeholders presented an issue in Sweden from the point of view of loss of control from centralization of current processes and also the need for clear frameworks of cooperation and incorporation of parties. Proskurovska & Dörry (2022) explain that the Swedish land registry which has all the centralized power over land administration would need to cede some control in order to work together with stakeholders along the transaction lifecycle. On the other hand, McMurren et al. (2018) describe that there is no clear framework of how this is supposed to happen and how cooperation between parties looks like. In order to scale the pilot project this would have to be defined.

Table 11: **Examples of "Government, Control and Cooperation" in Georgia**

GH	Baako et al., 2022	A critical analysis of the interviews revealed that directives implemented by the Lands Commission are not exempt from the influence of the executive arm of government, which is formed, and often dominated, by the political party in power. Essentially, the adoption or non-adoption of emerging technologies, such as Blockchain, for land administration in Ghana could be heavily impacted by the agenda of the government of the day, summed up in the concept of 'political will'. Where the political party that heads the government does not consider digitisation to be one of its priorities, the Lands Commission and other key sector agencies accordingly take a similar position.
GH	Zein & Twinomurinzi, 2023	However, this also presents challenges. BT poses a significant threat to established power structures within governments.
GH	Olsen, 2018	An interesting finding was the fact that none of the two companies interviewed was actively coordinating work or had a partnership with the Ghanaian government; they both worked independently with the communities in rural Ghana.

In Ghana problems relating to governmental will, control, and cooperation were also seen. On the one hand Baako et al. (2022) talks about the importance that the acting governments have on the implementation of new technologies basically saying that the agenda of the acting government has a big impact on whether or not new technologies are pursued and implemented. Add to that the idea that blockchain "poses a significant threat to established power structures within the government" (Zein & Twinomurinzi, 2023) and one can see that it is unlikely for it to be part of a governmental agenda. This lead to the situation as described by Olsen (2018) where neither of the companies (BenBen and Bitland) had an active partnership with the government. This poses problems to the implementation and scalability of the technology as the government could deem these activities as unlawful or not recognize them. "Legitimacy in the registration process in regard to conformity of formal rules for land registration is therefore debatable since neither have involved formal surveyors from the government." (Olsen, 2018)

Table 12: **Examples of "Government, Control and Cooperation" in Georgia**

IN	Kshetri, 2022	the uptake and use of new technologies hinge critically on intention, desire and commitment on the part of a government to carry through significant political reforms as well as the agreement of and support from state officials and other key actors.
IN	Kshetri, 2022	an inefficient bureaucracy has hampered the development and implementation of blockchain systems. As of August 2018, most blockchain projects in the AP had just completed the proof-of-concept (PoC) phase or were developing PoCs. Some government departments were not motivated to move beyond the PoC stage. There are also potential issues related to conflict and power relationships. In India, there has also been confusion regarding the central authority to handle blockchain systems.
IN	A. Sharma et al., 2021	Various agencies are involved in land registries such as Estate and sub registrar ofices; hence, many cumbersome pre-processes need to be completed to make a synchronous system.

In India Kshetri (2022) also identified that the implementation of new technologies hinges largely on the will of the politicians and their cooperation with other stakeholders to push through necessary legislations, such as for example the recognition of digital signatures as discussed in section 7.2.1 regarding LARF. But it was seen as described by Kshetri (2022) that most projects had not moved on past the proof of concept stages dues to the fact that there was no will to move past that stage. This could be a result of what A. Sharma et al. (2021) describes as "cumbersome pre-processes" that need to be completed to ensure cooperation between involved parties, but there is no will to go through with those cumbersome processes. Especially taking into consideration the "issues related to conflict and power" Kshetri (2022) where similarly to Ghana and Sweden blockchain would require a rearrangement of the power structures. Which would most likely be a hard sell on politicians.

To summarize the barrier of "Government, Control and Cooperation" across the cases where it was motioned, the success of blockchain implementation appears to be influenced not just by legal frameworks but also by the willingness of governments to cooperate, share control, and challenge existing power structures. Whether it is Sweden's centralized land authority, Ghana's influences of agendas of the acting governments, or India's stalled pilot projects, the lack of clear cooperation frameworks and political will has been a recurring barrier. With these structural and governance challenges in mind, the next barrier that will be analyzed is the quality of data and the condition of existing records.

7.2.3 Data Quality and Record Issues

Table 13: **Barrier Occurrence Matrix (DQARI)**

Sweden	Georgia	Ghana	India
		✓	✓

Table 14: **Examples of "Data Quality and Record Issues" in Ghana**

GH	Baako et al., 2022	The analysis further highlighted incomplete coverage of registration and digitalisation in the country. The Ghana Enterprise Land Information System (GELIS), which represents Ghana's prevailing effort towards digitalisation, covers circa 10 % of all land data in the country.
GH	Olsen, 2018	Finally, the lack of digitization stands as a dire reminder of why BCT should be evaluated on practical considerations and discussed in the context of the environment. The paper-based system is a major impediment for introducing a blockchain system and might indicate that the technology has been introduced too early as the instrument for breaking the poverty cycle in Sub Saharan Africa.
GH	Coleman, 2016	As Bitland works to transfer paper data into a digital format, it must also consolidate new land registry requests against the old registries, according to the project's white paper. In many cases, the official documents are outdated, and locals have their own ways to track titles. These problems must be solved to get a single registry that represents a consistent ledger of land title holdings.

Ghana had different problems regarding the data quality. For one, Baako et al. (2022) shows that in Ghana less than 10% of the land data is digitalized. This means that even if blockchain was theoretically implemented into the registry system, it would only cover a tenth of all the land in Ghana. This sentiment is carried also through Olsen (2018) who goes as far as saying that the feasibility of blockchain in Ghana's land registry should be evaluated on "practical considerations." The lack of digitalization and reliance on paper would not allow for blockchain to be implemented just purely from a practical point of view, let alone, political will, cooperation or any other of the barriers discussed. Working on digitalization is not as easy as just transferring existing record into digital databases, as (Coleman, 2016) describes, Bitland is facing problems while digitalizing records as official documents can be outdated, or locals have their own ways of tracking ownership.

Table 15: **Examples of "Data Quality and Record Issues" in India**

IN	Comincioli, 2021	A land-record system based on Blockchain request a high degree of certainty, the data uploaded on the blockchain cannot contain wrong information, neither they can contain transactions with disputes still pending, the problem in developing countries such as India, is that data regarding land properties and those regarding purchase and sale transactions present a certain frequency show discrepancy, this problem must be resolved before the blockchain is being implemented, if not the information uploaded will prove to be wrong
IN	Kshetri, 2022	Second, while blockchain systems are secure and trustworthy, their data – like that of other databases – are only as accurate as what is entered. In AP's case, some of the land records are reported to be of poor quality. Without clean records, blockchain's potential as a trust machine cannot be realised.
IN	P. Sharma et al., 2022	Due to the existence of poor quality land records, the introduction of blockchain to all land parcels is unsuitable.

This issue of data quality was not only seen in Ghana but also in India. Before blockchain can be implemented Comincioli (2021) writes that the problems about discrepancies shown in land and purchase data as well as transaction with pending disputes need to be resolved. Kshetri (2022) rightly states that the security of blockchain systems (as well as basic digitalization) is influenced by the accuracy of the data that goes into them. The importance of data quality cannot be understated and is so important that P. Sharma et al. (2022) goes as far as calling the use of blockchain unsuitable.

To wrap up the section on "Data Quality and Record Issues", even the most advanced blockchain system is only as good as the data it holds. In both Ghana and India, low levels of digitalization, outdated or conflicting records, and unresolved disputes severely limit the practical feasibility of implementing blockchain in land administration systems. These are not just technical obstacles, they are central to the theoretical security and benefits of blockchain, without quality data none of those can be achieved. With that in mind, the next section explores a more intangible but equally crucial barrier: how trust and perception shape the adoption of blockchain.

7.2.4 Trust and Perception

Table 16: **Barrier Occurrence Matrix (TAP)**

Sweden	Georgia	Ghana	India
✓	✓		✓

Table 17: **Examples of "Trust and Perception" in Sweden**

SE	Djursén & Björk, 2022	a large percentage has a great concern regarding regulatory uncertainty and a lack of trust among users
SE	Jonathan, 2021	While trust in digital contracts has been lagging for a long time, he argued that blockchain tech can now provide the trust needed to move forward. "As soon as the legislator understands that this is possible, I think it will come true," said Kempe.

The next barrier is one that plays a big role as users must have trust in the system or they will not want to participate in it, as has been discussed in the literature review. If there is a "lack of trust among users" (Djursén & Björk, 2022) as seen in the Swedish case the natural reaction would be to not use the system and stick to the systems that have worked in the past and are hence trusted. In an interview with Magnus Kempe from Kairos Future (the company which worked with the Swedish government on the pilot project) Jonathan (2021) writes that there has been no trust in digital contracts for a while. Kempe argues that this is no longer the case however the legislators seem to still not trust it. This brings another important facet to the trust barrier. It is not only the population that has to trust the system, but also the government who runs the system. Because if the government does not trust it, how could the population trust it?

Table 18: **Examples of "Trust and Perception" in Georgia**

GE	Aarvik, 2024	This, perhaps, explains why public perceptions around corruption have not continued to improve since blockchain was added to the registry.
GE	Aarvik, 2024	As we have seen, trust in the institutions handling the land registry is crucial; trust in the blockchain security layer, less so.

The case of Georgia is a prime example of the importance of trust. Even after the blockchain was introduced into the Georgian registry the public did not change their perception around corruption (Aarvik, 2024). Importantly, it was less about the technology itself and more about the trust in the institutions which are responsible of the land registration (Aarvik, 2024). Meaning that institutions should be trusted before any solution is implemented, be it blockchain based or paper based for that matter.

Table 19: **Examples of "Trust and Perception" in India**

IN	Bhattacharya, 2018	Having seen the government's dirty tricks, most of the farmers gathered at Rayapudi aren't buying the claim that the system is tamper-proof – especially at the stages before the information is moved to blockchain. After all, assignments and verifications are still being done by revenue officers on the ground.
IN	Bhattacharya, 2018	"The tampering cannot be stopped. If you give the right people a lot of bribe, they will go in and change the record," said Seshagiri Rao. Nearly $700 million is paid in bribes across land registrars in India, an Andhra Pradesh government official estimated last year, and even probes into these matters are often flawed.
IN	Kaushik, 2020	The land owners still have a fear of manipulation of records by those in charge of the data being transferred to the blockchain.
IN	Comincioli, 2021	The immutable nature of blockchain creates a sense of fear and distrust in the minds of employees and functionaries that will tend to continue to use existing computerized systems.

The importance of that last point on trust in institutions is clearly shown in the case study of India where farmers did not trusts the system, be it blockchain or not, due to the "government's dirty tricks" (Bhattacharya, 2018) in the past. These tricks are reflected in what one government official in Andhra Pradesh estimates to be around $700 million in land registry related bribes across India (Bhattacharya, 2018). On top of the bribes and other tricks, the population does not trust the government to truthfully transfer the data from current systems onto the blockchain system (Bhattacharya, 2018; Kaushik, 2020).

As before with the Swedish case the Indian case shows that it is not only the population that needs to trust the system but the government and the government employees too. Comincioli (2021) notes that the immutability of blockchain instills a sense of fear and distrust in government employees, which ultimately leads to them sticking to traditional and trusted systems that they know how to work with. The idea that people will trust that which they know and distrusts that which they do not. This idea is nothing new and it implies that trust can be gained through getting to know the system. In other words, through education of how the systems work, which is the next barrier that will be analyzed.

In short, trust (or the lack thereof) emerges as a major obstacle that represents a large barrier in the implementation of blockchain in land registries. Whether it is skepticism from the public due to past corruption from governments, or reluctance from governments and their employees to adopt a system they do not fully understand, the same dynamic keeps showing up: people fall back on what they know. This shows that trust is not just about the technology itself, but about the people running it and the experiences users have had with them. And if trust can be built through familiarity, then the role of education becomes critical. Which is exactly the barrier which the next section will dive into.

7.2.5 Education and Literacy

Table 20: **Barrier Occurrence Matrix (EAL)**

Sweden	Georgia	Ghana	India
✓		✓	✓

Table 21: **Example of "Education and Literacy" in Sweden**

SE	Jonsson, 2018	The first recommendation is to actively educate developers and decision makers about the technology.

In (Jonsson, 2018) discussion of recommendations of how to overcome barriers and implementing blockchain in the land registry, education is brought up. Interestingly he does not talk about the education of the general public but of those in charge of the projects and the developers working on it. Which makes sense. The key stakeholders driving the project need to understand the technology in order for them themselves to be able to educate the public on how it works and what the advantages of such a system are.

Table 22: **Examples of "Education and Literacy" in Ghana**

GH	Ameyaw & de Vries, 2023	Public-stakeholder acceptance is however dependent on their awareness, and understanding of the technology.
GH	Baako et al., 2022	Finally, the analysis yielded low levels of digital literacy as a potential barrier to the adoption of BCT in Ghana. This is consistent with findings by Ehwi and Asante (2016) that land sector professionals need to upgrade their digital literacy if any digitisation efforts will see significant success.
GH	Baako et al., 2022	There are also several misconceptions associated with land registration in general in Ghana which will translate to BCT. Many Ghanaians, per our interviews, do not use title registration because they think it is reserved for the elite. The analysis shows that many middle-class real estate transacting parties do not see the usefulness of land registration, except as a way in which highly educated and "bookish" individuals flaunt their property ownership status. Not wanting to associate with this kind of perception, the former group desists from land registration, affecting land registration uptake.

Ameyaw & de Vries (2023) give more insights on the relationship between understanding and trust that was previously spoken about in the TAP section. They describe how the public's acceptance of the technology is predicated on their understanding of the technology. Furthermore, education and particularly digital literacy are also identified in the Ghanian case study as a potential barrier (Baako et al., 2022). This again highlights the importance of digital education and most importantly the understanding of the technologies which are being implemented.

Talking about a different aspect of education, which indirectly leads to problems with implementing blockchain in land registries is the misconception that were witnessed in Ghana by some members of the public, regarding land registries in general. Baako et al. (2022) found that many Ghanaians do not make use of land registrations as they think these are things only the elite make use of in order to show off the fact that they own a building. So, in order not to be associated with such behaviors people choose not to deal with land registries. The problem of this specific barrier is that education in the sense of teaching these people what the benefits of using the land registry would probably intensify their feeling that this is only for "educated and bookish individuals" (Baako et al., 2022).

Table 23: **Examples of "Education and Literacy" in India**

IN	Kumar & Motwani, 2025	Education and Training: Education and training of key government officials and other people involved in the process are necessary for a successful use of the blockchain technology in the land registry. This means that they have to be theoretical concerns about the technology, its benefits and how its limitations could be addressed.
IN	A. Sharma et al., 2021	Even the implementing departments may face human resource constraints while working on this technology. At present the numbers of blockchain developers are meager in the world. The requisite experts of blockchain technology are in short supply, at least in India.
IN	Comincioli, 2021	a lack of experts specialized in the implementation of blockchain's architectures, the experts familiar with the different types (private, public, hybrid) of blockchains were and are still limited.
IN	Comincioli, 2021	A limited number of governmental and private organizations whit the requested prerequisites to work and carry-out a successful training for public employees and administrators.

In the Indian case study education was also identified as a barrier in different ways. On the one side there is a lack of education and of trained professionals. But on the other side there is a lack of trained people who can teach and educate the rest. Kumar & Motwani (2025) identified education as being a necessary requirement for blackchins use. Comincioli (2021) talks about the lack of experts available who are specialized in the creation and implementation of different types of blockchains. This sentiment is also identified by A. Sharma et al. (2021) who say that these types of experts are in "short supply,(...) in India." But the biggest problem is identified by Comincioli (2021) who says that there is a lack of "governmental and private organizations" with the wherewithal to successfully educate those very experts all the other literature say are needed so badly.

Summing up the "Education and literacy" Barrier, it shows up in several layers. It is not just about educating the public, but also about whether the people leading these projects, and those meant to build them, actually understand what they are working with. Without that foundational knowledge, trust cannot be built, adoption will be severely slowed down, and misconceptions can spread further slowing down the process. Even when the will to educate is there, a shortage of experts and institutions to train them poses its own education barrier. With all that said, even the best-educated team cannot overcome certain limits if the technology itself is not ready. The next section will therefore look at the technical limitations of blockchain technology as it was observed in the case studies.

7.2.6 Technical Limitations

Table 24: **Barrier Occurrence Matrix (TL)**

Sweden	Georgia	Ghana	India
✓	✓		✓

Table 25: **Examples of "Technical Limitations" in Sweden**

SE	McMurren et al., 2018	In addition, security provisions built into legacy systems have prevented further digitization of the land transfer process, for example by imposing restrictions through firewalls and limits on network connections. As a result, while some institutional actors (including realtors, banks, and some government agencies) could connect their systems to Lantmäteriet databases, individual buyers and sellers could not.
SE	Garcia-Teruel, 2020	Current projects, which focus on blockchain and the use of smart contracts, allow the owner to sell the property while this transaction is registered at the same time. This is the case of the Landmateriet in Sweden and other projects from private initiatives such as Velow.re. However, the range of rights that can created and registered in land registers is wider in practice. It might be difficult to translate certain rights into the code of a smart contract, both rights in rem and even the clauses of a tenancy contract.

In Sweden two types of technical limitations were identified as barriers, one was of the existing digital system (legacy systems) and the other was a limitation in the functionality of smart contracts.

McMurren et al. (2018) talk about the problem with limitations in the legacy systems, where things such as firewalls and network connection limits built into the systems originally as security provisions are now limiting the expansion of digitalization. This is similar to the problems previously discussed in the Ghana and India cases where limitations to current digitalization efforts lead to difficulties in developing the blockchain solutions.

The limitations regarding smart contract functionality is analyzed by Garcia-Teruel (2020). She describes the problem as being one where the current functionality of smart contracts is enough to allow for simple transactions.

However, when it comes to a larger range of rights that in practice can be created through registries, the smart contracts start to fall short, and it becomes more complicated. For example, rights in rem and specific tenancy contract clauses.

Table 26: **Examples of "Technical Limitations" in Georgia**

GE	v. Weizsäcker et al., 2018	The small-scale solution of timestamping transactions of existing land registries by writing hashes on a public ledger is relatively straightforward and easy to implement. Yet, the more disruptive solution in which land transactions are executed in a fully automated manner through the use of smart contracts, faces significant implementation hurdles
GE	v. Weizsäcker et al., 2018	Firstly, land titles and obligations are often complex and involve additional information beyond the identity of the land tenant. For instance, mechanisms and procedures have to be defined for land seizure in cases of insolvency etc. Projecting such complex modalities of rules and obligations into a blockchain will require not only careful and thorough coding of smart contracts but also institutions to go through a significant adaptation of their management processes.

7

This idea of limited functionality of smart contracts was also found to have been mentioned in relation to the Georgian case. According to v. Weizsäcker et al. (2018) current functionality such as timestamping existing land registries is a relatively straightforward functionality that blockchain can do, but that fully automated solutions using smart contracts still faces hurdles. Similar to what was said about smart contracts in the Swedish case. They then go on to say that land titles and obligations are not that simple and that their proper implementation into smart contracts would need a significant change in the way that institutions manage the land registry system.

Table 27: **Examples of "Technical Limitations" in India**

IN	Bhattacharya, 2018	This addition of a middle-man can throw a spanner in the works even for a relatively hack-proof technology like blockchain. "Land registries generally speaking won't make too much sense if you still have a government office in the middle which you need to trust in order to transfer property," said Markos Zachariadis, associate professor at Warwick Business

		School and a fintech research fellow at the University of Cambridge. Of course, it helps if a record is lost or tampered with, or damaged in a natural disaster. But it does little to curb manipulation by those in charge of the data being transferred to the blockchain.
IN	Kshetri, 2022	Finally, the experiences of government blockchain projects in AP and other Indian states have shown that the migration and integration of legacy IT and database management systems into a blockchain-based system would be a difficult task. A major barrier is that different systems from which data need to be transferred to the blockchain system use different data formats and models. The integration of diverse data and systems into blockchain platforms could be costly and time consuming.

In the Indian case a barrier relating to technical limitations was identified which is in line with some of the sentiments mentioned in the literature review such as (Zheng et al., 2017), that the power of blockchain comes from its decentralization capabilities, but that such a system of a land registry is unthinkable and that it would most likely be a private or permissioned system, where the aspect of decentralization is lost. As Markos Zachariadis (associate professor at Warwick Business School and a fintech research fellow at the University of Cambridge), quoted by Bhattacharya (2018) says that in the realm of land registries an implementation of blockchain does not make much sense as one still needs to trust the central authority of the government to transfer a property. In other words, whether it is a current digital system or a blockchain system the power still lays with the government.

The other aspect of technical limitations in the Indian case study relates to the different technologies and datatypes that are currently used and how merging them all into a blockchain system "would be costly and time consuming" (Kshetri, 2022).

Summarizing the section on "Technical Limitations", while blockchain is often praised for its potential, the reality is that the technology currently has some limits. Whether it is legacy systems with outdated architecture, the restricted functionality of smart contracts, or the fact that a truly decentralized land registry seems practically unworkable, these technical challenges show that not everything is ready to be replaced or reimagined just yet. Even if all other barriers were removed, the tech itself might not yet be fit for purpose. And beyond what the technology can or cannot do, there is another very basic but crucial layer to consider: the infrastructure needed to run it. That is what the next section will focus on.

7.2.7 Infrastructure Limitations

Table 28: **Barrier Occurrence Matrix (IL)**

Sweden	Georgia	Ghana	India
		✓	✓

Table 29: **Examples of "Infrastructure Limitations" in Ghana**

GH	Ameyaw & de Vries, 2023	Thus, avenues for a stable electricity power support are an important consideration for blockchain adoption.
GH	Baako et al., 2022	A dominant concern raised by all respondents to the study was one of inadequate infrastructure to support the use of the technology. Erratic power supply coupled with limited cyber infrastructure and usage across the country featured significantly in the interview data. Respondents posited that unreliable power supply significantly disrupted economic activity hence the fortunes of Blockchain technology adoption remain similarly bleak.
GH	Coleman, 2016	Bitland cannot, however, rely on existing local infrastructure solely on account of "rolling blackouts," a big problem in Ghana. The infrastructure is unreliable in many areas. There are 24- to 48- hour periods where large areas go without electricity. Hence, electronic solutions would not be feasible unless there were a failsafe as part of the ecosystem.

One barrier which may not spring to mind at first but becomes logical once one thinks about it is the technical and connectivity infrastructure. In Ghana this is a major consideration for the adoption of blockchain as described by Ameyaw & de Vries (2023). Baako et al. (2022) takes it a step further and calls blockchains outlooks "bleak" due to the unstable power supply and the fact that cyber infrastructure is not greatly developed in Ghana. This is also touched on by (Coleman, 2016) who says that Bitland faced problems with blackouts and that large areas of the country go 24 to 48 hours without any electricity. For a solution that relies heavily on the constant running of computers, it cannot go for such periods without energy. Hence the ecosystem has to also incorporate fail safes (Coleman, 2016).

Table 30: **Examples of "Infrastructure Limitations" in India**

IN	Comincioli, 2021	The set-up of a network with enough bandwidth to keep the nodes running is not simple. The availability of networks in India is still quite low.
IN	P. Sharma et al., 2022	Considering the scale-up at the state or national level,the central cloud servers become an issue and thus may be a great failure point that can distort the total network.
IN	Kshetri, 2022	a large proportion of the state's population lacks Internet access. As of January 2021, AP's Internet penetration was 31 %, which was below the national average of 36 %.

India's infrastructure limitations relate more to the availability of enough bandwidth to keep the blockchain nodes running (Comincioli, 2021). These limitations could be a problem when scaling up the solutions at the state or national levels at which point the available cloud servers would become an issue (P. Sharma et al., 2022). But also generally the availability of internet in the State in which the case study was carried out is lacking, Kshetri (2022) says that the internet penetration in Andhra Pradesh is less than the national average of 36%. These limitations would not allow large scale implementation of blockchain in India.

Concluding this section about the "Infrastructure Limitations", without stable access to electricity, internet, and the necessary tech infrastructure, even the best blockchain system is not likely to succeed. As seen in Ghana and India, the basic requirements to keep such a system running, reliable power, consistent connectivity, and server capacity, are still not guaranteed. These are not just minor inconveniences but make or break barriers that need to be addressed before any meaningful implementation can take place. That said, sometimes it is not about what can or cannot be done, but rather about what people in power are willing to let happen. The next section will explore how the preservation of the status quo by those who benefit from it can become a barrier in and of itself.

7.2.8 Preservation of Status Quo

Table 31: **Barrier Occurrence Matrix (POSQ)**

Sweden	Georgia	Ghana	India
✓		✓	

Table 32: **Example of "Preservation of Status Quo" in Sweden**

SE	Djursén & Björk, 2022	Another challenge found in the interview with Renström is that information asymmetry in a transaction can be beneficial for an experienced buyer or seller. The reason is that those opportunities and risks can come from information asymmetry, which would mean that some actors in the market would be reluctant to adopt the technology. Since they otherwise could capitalize on the information asymmetry.

The blockchain technology and its promise of transparency as talked about in the literature review would as described by Djursén & Björk (2022) not be a welcome addition by those market participants that seek to capitalize on the very fact that information asymmetry exists in Sweden. These kinds of experienced buyer and seller would not want to adopt the changes.

Table 33: **Examples of "Preservation of Status Quo" in Ghana**

GH	Ameyaw, 2024	Possibility of chiefs, as well as some public land sector officials, to undermine any system that will try to make their activities more transparent and accountable
GH	Ameyaw & de Vries, 2021	It is essential to mention that threats of system sabotage from some corrupt land officials, and customary authorities who might not wish for transparency in their deals, exist.
GH	Baako et al., 2022	Another potential barrier to the adoption of BCT, and other technologies, in Ghana is the socio-cultural barrier of information hoarding. Generally, Ghanaians are very private with their information and avoid sharing information about property transactions. People simply do not want others to know about their ownership. The risk, perceived or real, of technology making public transactional data may dissuade Ghanaians from adopting the technology. This information "hoarding" persists despite the benefits of data transparency. This high

		level of sensitivity and anonymity that users in Ghana attach to real estate transactions has been captured in previous studies including Baako (2019).

In Ghana the resistance to change would not come from experienced market participants seeking a profit. But from the people in power who currently benefit from the inefficient process and members of the public concerned with the privacy of their real estate ownership. Ameyaw & de Vries (2021) as well as Ameyaw (2024) both describe similar ideas that corrupt public sector officials and customary authorities could undermine or sabotage any system that seeks to shed more transparency into the real estate transactions. As this would also shed light into their dealings and activities which they likely would prefer to stay hidden.

Baako et al. (2022) discusses a sociocultural aspect in Ghana where people attach great importance in anonymity regarding real estate transactions. This, Baako goes on to say, is due to the fact that "people simply do not want others to know about their ownership." Any technology which has a risk of exposing these ownerships is not likely to catch on with Ghanaians, whether the risk is real or only perceived (Baako et al., 2022).

Summing up this section on "Preservation of Status Quo", it becomes clear that not everyone would benefit from greater transparency, at least not in their eyes. Whether it is corrupt officials, traditional authorities, or even private individuals worried about exposing ownership, those who gain from the existing systems in place often have the strongest incentive to keep things as they are. And when resistance is built into the structure itself, even the best intentions can fall flat. That is why it is useful to also look at where things have worked. The next section will take a closer look at the success factors that emerged in the Georgian case study.

7.3 Success Factors

While doing the analysis and coding cycles for all the papers a trend started to emerge with the Georgian case study. Many of the papers that made it into analysis stage had made it because they did indeed discuss problems, but often times they were not related to the specific Georgian case study. A choice had to be made. Whether to drop the Georgian case studies and continue with the other three or to continue analyzing it in hopes to find more problems and barriers that can be analyzed. Ultimately the choice was made to include it in the research not only because it did show barrier, even if few, but more importantly because interestingly the barriers that were being found in other case studies were coming up in the Georgian papers as success factors. This was an interesting contrast and would add value to the barriers that were found as it showed the opposite side of the barriers. In other words, it showed that these barriers if worked on can become success factors.

This section is dedicated to those. It will show what was found in the Georgian case study as success factors and it will contrast this with the prior analysis that has been carried out. To begin the table below shows the success factors as they were coded in the first cycle code. It is worth repeating, that even if they can be found inside the coding matrix in Appendix 1 they have all been removed from the calculations and charts in the first section of the analysis so as to not mix the barriers with the success factors.

Table 34: **Success factor 1st Cycle Codes Georgia**

Codes
Legislative framework regarding data – success factor
Vital Public-private cooperation – success factor
Data quality – success factor
Education – success factor
Private and Public Digital literacy – success factor
Importance of e-government – success factor

7.3.1 Legislative Data Framework and Data Quality

Table 35: **Examples of "Legislative Data Framework and Data Quality" in Georgia**

GE	Lazuashvili et al., 2019	The legislative framework is a crucial aspect for the successful integration of blockchain technology. In case of Georgia, the project success is greatly determined by the flexibility of the respective regulations that do not hinder NAPR from saving the citizens' data on the blockchain. In cases of other countries such as Sweden or The Netherlands, for administering blockchain technology into the public service, major regulatory changes are required.
GE	Shang & Price, 2019	The success of the Georgia project was the result of two crucial elements – education and data quality.
GE	Shang & Price, 2019	More importantly, the existence of high-quality data helped guarantee the validity of the project. Without accurate data, the power of a Blockchain-based solution for a land registry would have been greatly limited, as poor-quality information posted on the Blockchain would make third-party verification of land titles difficult.

This section combines the "Legislative framework regarding data – success factor" and the "Data quality – success factor" and looks at them as one as the quality of data and the legal framework surrounding it go hand in hand in the Georgian case study.

Lazuashvili et al. (2019) start by explaining how the flexibility that was given to the National Agency of Public Registry (NAPR) in terms of regulations regarding the storage of citizens data on the blockchain. This flexibility, they say, is a contributing factor to the successful integration of blockchain.

This freedom to operate which also gives them clarity on how to deal with the data is the opposite of what has been discussed in the Swedish case study, where scalability remains a challenge due the fact that "Frameworks for data governance (...) must still be defined" (McMurren et al., 2018).

On the other side of this success factor Shang & Price (2019) discuss the importance of data quality and how it was one of two elements which contributed to the success of the Georgian project. They say that in order to benefit from the full "power" of blockchain solutions the data has to be accurate and high quality, which it was in Georgia. The importance of high-quality data was discussed as a central barrier in both the Ghanaian case and the Indian case, where existing paper based systems lack data quality which makes it hard for it to be integrated into a blockchain-based system (Coleman, 2016; Olsen, 2018; Kshetri, 2022; P. Sharma et al., 2022).

7.3.2 Public – Private Cooperation

Table 36: **Examples of "Public – Private Cooperation" in Georgia**

GE	Aarvik, 2024	Sustained public-private partnership was beneficial in Georgia.
GE	Lazuashvili et al., 2019	Public-private partnership is a crucial aspect for blockchain-technology adoption. In case of Georgia, the Bitfury group develops the blockchain solution for the government and since then keeps providing the service. The same applies to other adopter countries as well where occasionally even several privatesector companies provide the solutions for integrating blockchain technology into existing land-registry systems.
GE	Lazuashvili et al., 2019	Besides the aspiration for Gerogia to portray a high e-governance development standard, reducing project risk for the government by initiating public-private cooperation is identified as a major incentive. Additionally, in the Georgian case, costs of the project along with the technology maintenance expenditures are covered by the private blockchain service-provider company.

Moving on the to the importance of cooperation between private stakeholders and the government. The idea of cooperation is evident both in (Aarvik, 2024) and (Lazuashvili et al., 2019) who both highlight how this partnership benefited and was a crucial aspect of the blockchain implementation project. This cooperation also serves for the government as a way to reduce the project risk and distribute who will carry the costs of its development and maintenance, which in the Case of Georgia is the private sector (Lazuashvili et al., 2019).

Thinking back to the analysis of the barriers encountered particularly in Ghana regarding cooperation it is clear to see why this theme is crucial. On the one side there is full private and public cooperation splitting risks and cost burdens and on the other side there are private companies working on the solution without the support of the government as seen in Ghana (Olsen, 2018) which leads to problems such as legal recognition or blockchain records and data issues. Things that Bitfury did not have to worry about as they cooperated with the government.

7.3.3 Education and Digital Literacy

Table 37: **Examples of "Education and Digital Literacy" in Georgia**

GE	v. Weizsäcker et al., 2018	Lastly, digital infrastructure and literacy are pre-requirements for implementing a blockchain-based land registry system. This applies to both authorities as well as citizens.
GE	Shang & Price, 2019	The success of the Georgia project was the result of two crucial elements – education and data quality.
GE	Shang & Price, 2019	For a Blockchain-based project to succeed, all stakeholders must be educated about Blockchain technology and the challenges it can address. Tomicah Tillemann, founder of the Blockchain Trust Accelerator, said of the Georgia project that "education and public engagement are as crucial as the technical side of the work. Technology is not going to take care of itself. People and the government need to know why they are using this technology and what problem it can solve." Throughout the project, the NAPR helped the Georgian people understand how Blockchain technology can ensure the immutability of land title data without sacrificing privacy

This section combines the success factors "Private and Public Digital literacy – success factor" and "Education – success factor" under one combined Education and Digital Literacy factor which closer resembles the barrier theme identified as EAL in the analysis.

V. Weizsäcker et al. (2018) begin by laying out the importance of digital literacy for building successful blockchain-based systems, going as far as calling it a pre-requirement. They further specify that this is the case both for the authorities in charge but also the citizens. Shang & Price (2019) also speaks about education in similar terms who call education one of two contributing factors to the success of the project in Georgia. They go further to describe that the NAPR not only focused on the technical aspects of the project but throughout it they also helped "the Georgian people understand how Blockchain technology can ensure the immutability of land title data without sacrificing privacy" (Shang & Price, 2019).

This idea of teaching how the blockchain keeps records safe is precisely one of the barriers identified in Ghana where people worried that the technology could lay open their property ownerships (Baako et al., 2022). Additionally this idea of education both in those running the system but also in the population was a barrier touched upon both in the India case and in the Swedish case (Jonsson, 2018; A. Sharma et al., 2021; Comincioli, 2021; Kumar & Motwani, 2025).

7.3.4 Importance of E-Government

Table 38: **Examples of "Importance of E-Government" in Georgia**

GE	Aarvik, 2024	A developed e-Government service is a prerequisite.
GE	Lazuashvili et al., 2019	Having a developed e-government is one of the biggest benefits to face the challenge of blockchain adoption. This element is also identified as a major support factor for the successful implementation of the Georgian land-titling project. Based on international rankings, Georgia shows significant results in the advancement of e-government development as also previously also discussed in the extended version of this paper.

Last but not least, the importance of a developed E-government. In the UN's annual report on E-Government which tracks the global developments in this topic through their E-Government Development Index (EGDI) Georgia had scored the title of "Very high EDGI" (*UN E-Government Survey 2024*, 2024) which puts it among the highest scoring countries. Aarvik (2024) discusses the importance of a developed e-government as being a prerequisite for the success that blockchain has had in Georgia. He mentions that not only was it a prerequisite but it was also identified as a "criteria for a successful implementation of this technology in government projects" (Aarvik, 2024). Lazuashvili et al. (2019) build on the importance of having a developed e-government for the implementation of blockchain. In fact they call it "the biggest benefit to face the challenge of blockchain adoption" (Lazuashvili et al., 2019) and also say that it is a major contributing factor to the success of the blockchain pilot project.

Together, these four success factors show why Georgia's blockchain land registry pilot was comparatively successful. The combination of a flexible legislative framework and high-quality data gave the project both clarity and a solid foundation, two elements that were missing or underdeveloped in the other case studies. Public–private cooperation ensured risk and cost-sharing, while digital literacy and public education efforts made the technology more accessible and less intimidating. Lastly, a well-developed e-government infrastructure helped tie everything together, creating an environment that could realistically support such an innovation. When viewed against the barriers encountered in Sweden, India, and Ghana, these factors don't just explain Georgia's relative success, they highlight what might be needed elsewhere to make similar projects work. With this in mind, the following conclusion wraps up the main findings of this research, reflects on the implications for future land registry modernization efforts, and considers the broader role blockchain could play in shaping public digital infrastructure.

8 Conclusion

8

In conclusion, having now looked at each of the individual case studies and analyzed them side by side, it is time to draw the research to a close and make sense of what was found. The goal here is not to repeat everything that has already been said, but to piece it all together and see what the bigger picture looks like. Throughout this research, two key research questions were laid out, and the aim was to explore them through the lens of actual blockchain implementation attempts in land registries. These were not theoretical wish lists but real-world examples where people rolled up their sleeves and tried to make something work. What came out of that is a rather clear picture of where things tend to fall apart, and also, where they can succeed.

First off, no matter which country you looked at, there was always some issue with the legal and regulatory framework. Sometimes it was the lack of recognition for digital signatures, other times it was the vague legal status of smart contracts, but the point is: the law just has not caught up to the technology yet. This was true in Sweden, Georgia, Ghana, and India. So even if the technical side was ready, the legal side often holds everything back. And what is interesting is that even in countries where the law theoretically allowed certain changes, like Ghana, things did not move forward because of how people behaved in practice, paper was still the proffered way to go.

Government willingness and cooperation also turned out to be make-or-break factors. In Sweden, you had one agency sitting on a lot of power and not quite ready to share it or the frameworks of how to share it were not quite clear. In Ghana and India, it came down to political will, whether or not the people in charge even cared to push for change. And importantly, if the successive acting governments were willing to continue the push. Blockchain can sound exciting on paper, but in reality, it often challenges existing

P. L. Reiser et al., *Blockchain in Global Land Registries*,
https://doi.org/10.1007/978-3-658-50076-4_8

power structures, and those in charge are not exactly lining up to dismantle their own influence.

Data quality was another major roadblock. This was especially clear in Ghana and India, where most records are not even digitized. And it is not just about scanning old papers, some of the data is wrong, incomplete, or being disputed. Since blockchain locks information in once it is in the system, putting bad data on a blockchain just locks in the mess. By now most people know the old adage "garbage in, garbage out" and here it could not ring truer. Without good input, the benefits of the technology cannot be realized.

Then there is the issue of trust. Trust in the system, trust in the institutions running it, and even trust within the government itself. In India, years of corruption meant that people simply did not believe the new system would be any better than the old one. In Sweden, it was not even about the people, it was the lawmakers who did not trust digital contracts. It is not hard to see why: people and institutions stick to what they know, especially when the new thing feels abstract or risky.

This ties directly into the next barrier, education and literacy. One cannot trust what one does not understand. And in many cases, people did not understand how blockchain works, what it does, or why it is supposedly better than existing systems. But it was not just the public, governments did not have enough trained experts either. There were not enough people who could build the systems, and even fewer who could teach others how to use them.

On the technical side, blockchain itself still lacks behind what the real world would need from it. For one, smart contracts are still limited in what they can do particularly when it comes to more intricate aspects of real estate related contracts (such as rights in rem and specific tenancy agreements). Another point was that legacy systems, especially in Sweden, created headaches for integration. And even if the tech were ready, the lack of infrastructure in countries like Ghana and parts of India (power outages and poor internet) means the whole thing becomes unfeasible.

And do not forget perhaps the least talked about, but possibly most powerful barrier of them all: people who benefit from the current system not wanting to see it change. Whether it is corrupt officials in Ghana or individuals who prefer their property dealings to stay private, the status quo is deeply rooted. And blockchain, with its transparency, shakes that up. So of course, there is pushback.

But it is not all bad news. The Georgian case shows us that success is possible. There, a few things were done differently: the legal framework was made flexible, public-private cooperation was prioritized, and digital literacy was treated as a core part of the rollout, not an afterthought. Add to that a functioning e-government system and good data, and you have a real shot at making blockchain work. Georgia proved that many of the barriers seen elsewhere are not immovable, they can be flipped into success factors when done right. Now, going back to the research questions to see how they held up.

RQ1: "What are the common challenges in implementing blockchain-based land administration/registry systems, and what lessons can be learned from past cases?"

The common challenges turned out to be legal ambiguity, lack of political will and cooperation, poor data quality, low levels of trust, insufficient education and literacy, technical limitations, infrastructure issues, and resistance from those benefiting from the status quo. Each of these was encountered in at least two case studies. The lesson? Technology alone will not fix anything. Success comes from building solid legal frameworks, cleaning up the data, educating all parties involved, and creating systems people can actually trust. None of which will happen by accident. It has to be intentional.

RQ2: "Are similar roadblocks to blockchain implementation in land registries observable across jurisdictions?"

Yes, absolutely. While every country had its own mix of these challenges, the core barriers repeated themselves. Legal issues, political resistance, bad data, lack of trust, these themes came up again and again. That consistency tells us that these are not isolated barriers, but systemic patterns. And that means future efforts can prepare for them in advance, no matter the country.

In the end, the answer to "Why has blockchain not been adopted in land registries?" is not a single answer. It is a mix of interrelated problems, technical, legal, social, and political. But now that they have been mapped out, the road ahead is at least a little clearer.

9 Recommendations

Now that the barriers have been laid out and the case studies compared, the next logical step is to ask: what can actually be done about it? It is one thing to say a system did not work because of legal, political, or technical problems it is another thing entirely to start identifying what future attempts should do differently. This section aims to at least shed some light in that regard. It does not pretend to give a one-size-fits-all solution, because frankly, there is not one. But based on what was seen across the case studies, there are certain themes and points that future projects should probably keep in mind if they are serious about making blockchain work in land administration.

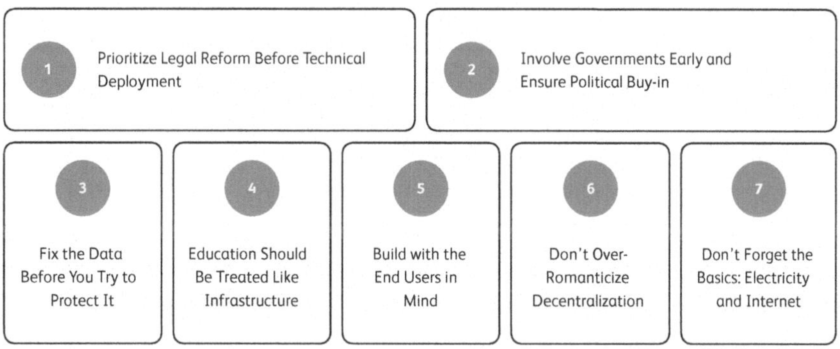

Figure 6: **Recommendations for blockchain implementation in land registries**

P. L. Reiser et al., *Blockchain in Global Land Registries*,
https://doi.org/10.1007/978-3-658-50076-4_9

9.1 Prioritize Legal Reform Before Technical Deployment

One of the clearest takeaways from the research is that without proper legal backing, no blockchain-based system is going to make it very far. It does not matter if the system works perfectly on a technical level, if the law still demands paper signatures or does not recognize smart contracts, then that system will not experience widespread adoption. This was seen in Sweden, Georgia, India, and Ghana, all to varying degrees.

So instead of jumping straight into pilot projects, countries should first look at their own laws and ask: Do we even allow for digital transactions in land transfers? Is there legal clarity on digital identities, signatures, and contract enforcement? If the answer is no, then that is where the work has to begin. There is no point trying to digitalize a system that is still legally stuck in the 20th century.

9.2 Involve Governments Early and Ensure Political Buy-in

This might sound obvious, but it clearly is not being done enough: governments need to be involved, not just as a rubber-stamping authority at the end of the project but from day one. In Ghana and India, for example, private companies tried to build systems without full government support. And surprise, it did not work. Without political buy-in, projects either get blocked, ignored, or quietly die out.

On the flip side, Georgia showed how things can look when the government is actually involved and working together with private partners. When responsibilities, costs, and benefits are shared or at least clearly attributed to a party, the result is much more stable. Governments should not see themselves as the customer, they should see themselves as co-builders.

9.3 Fix the Data Before You Try to Protect It

Another recurring theme is that poor data quality completely kills the promise of blockchain. This was especially obvious in Ghana and India. It is easy to think that blockchain is a fix-all solution, but it is not magic. If the data going into the blockchain is wrong, missing, or disputed, then the whole idea of immutability just locks in errors. And once data is in the blockchain, it cannot be easily changed due to the very nature of the technology.

So, before a single line of code is written for a blockchain pilot, the basic land records need to be cleaned up. That includes digitizing them, resolving disputes, and getting rid of conflicting or outdated entries. Otherwise, one would just be creating a digital version of a broken system.

9.4 Education Should Be Treated Like Infrastructure

One thing that came up repeatedly, both in the literature and in interviews, was the issue of trust. And tied into that was the issue of understanding. People do not trust what they do not understand. It is really that simple. Whether it was the Swedish lawmakers hesitant about digital signatures or the Indian farmers mistrusting data transfers, the barrier was often more psychological than technical.

This is where education comes in, not as a side project but as a central part of any blockchain implementation. People need to understand what blockchain is, what it does, and how it affects them. And it is not just the public, government employees, registry staff, and even the developers themselves need to be trained properly. A big problem, especially in India, was simply the lack of experts who understood the systems they were meant to build. If nobody really gets how the system works, how can it ever be trusted? Education should therefore not be seen as a "soft" side activity but as core infrastructure, just like servers or power grids.

9.5 Build with the End Users in Mind

Another key insight, especially from Ghana, is that even if you build the perfect system, people might just not use it. Some did not see the point of registering land in the first place, others were afraid it would expose them. And the more digital and complex the system gets, the more alienating it becomes for people who already feel outside of the formal system.

So, one recommendation here is simple: avoid designing the system for the ideal user. Design it for the actual user. That means taking into account social norms, local practices, and cultural attitudes toward land ownership. And it means building something that feels accessible, not intimidating. The system has to work for everyone, not just for the "educated and bookish".

9.6 Don't Over-Romanticize Decentralization

A bit of honesty is needed here too. Blockchain sounds good on paper, but it does not always do what people think it does. In land administration, for example, the whole idea of decentralization starts to fall apart. Because at the end of the day, you still need the state to back the transfer of land rights. That means some central authority is always going to be involved. And if that is the case, maybe a full decentralized public blockchain is not even the right fit. Maybe a permissioned or hybrid system makes more sense. This is not about giving up on blockchain, it is about using the right tool for the job. There is no point forcing full decentralization if what you really need is accountability and interoperability with state systems.

9.7 Don't Forget the Basics: Electricity and Internet

Last but not least, it is worth pointing out that blockchain systems don not run on hopes and dreams. They need power, bandwidth, and hardware. And in countries where blackouts are common or where internet coverage is patchy, this becomes a real problem. Ghana was a perfect example of this. It is easy to talk about trustless systems and immutability, but if the server shuts down every other day, none of that matters.

Any plan to implement blockchain has to first check: do we even have the infrastructure to support it? If not, then either the infrastructure needs to be upgraded, or the project needs to be scaled back to match what is actually doable.

10 Critical Reflection

Like most research projects, this work comes with its fair share of limitations, some expected, others that became clear only as the work progressed. One of the biggest issues had to do with the availability and quality of sources. While there is plenty of writing out there on blockchain in land administration, much of it focuses on the upsides: the benefits, the potential, and the theory. There is far less on what actually went wrong in real-life projects and that's a problem when the whole point of this research was to understand exactly that.

Particularly challenging was the fact that many papers barely touched on the problems at all, even when discussing known pilot projects. Instead, they often focused on how blockchain could help, without saying much about what happened when someone actually tried to use it. This might be because the people writing those papers were close to the projects themselves, developers, sponsors, or even government agencies, and naturally had an interest in making the tech look good. It's not hard to see why someone would want to focus on the upside when pitching a new system, but it leaves a gap in the literature and makes proper analysis harder.

The Georgia case is a good example. While it's often cited as one of the most successful examples of blockchain in land administration, finding detailed and critical reflections on the project was surprisingly difficult. Much of the available material focused on celebrating its success rather than exploring its challenges. In the end, it was decided to keep Georgia as one of the case studies anyway, because it offered a valuable counterpoint to the others, namely, that of showing what factors can lead to success. But it's worth acknowledging that the depth of insight one could gather about specific barriers in the

P. L. Reiser et al., *Blockchain in Global Land Registries*,
https://doi.org/10.1007/978-3-658-50076-4_10

Georgian case doesn't quite match what was available for Sweden, Ghana, or India.

There are also some limitations on the methodological side. The method used for this research was qualitative cross-case analysis, which is a great tool for identifying recurring patterns across different situations. However, this approach is only as good as the data it relies on. If the data is limited, biased, or incomplete, as it sometimes was here, then the patterns that emerge might not tell the full story. While the point of using multiple types of sources (journal articles, reports, interviews, and official statements) was made, the fact is that some topics just didn't have as much solid documentation as others.

Another limitation worth mentioning is selection bias. The case studies were selected heavily based on the availability of source material. That means some relevant examples may have been left out simply because they weren't well-documented in English or didn't offer enough detail for proper analysis. Similarly, within each case study, only certain perspectives made it into the final cut, often those that were easier to find or better documented. This could mean that some stakeholders' voices are underrepresented.

There is also a limitation concerning coding reliability. All coding and theme identification were carried out without inter-coder verification. While the use of MAXQDA helped maintain consistency across the coding process, there was no triangulation with additional coders or peer checks. This means that the thematic categories and interpretations are subject to bias, however unintentional. Future studies could strengthen the reliability of findings by involving multiple coders or including feedback loops to validate emerging patterns.

On top of that, there's the question of how broadly the findings can be applied. This research does not claim to speak for every country or context. Land administration is highly context-specific, and blockchain projects are influenced by everything from legal traditions to political will and local infrastructure. What works (or fails) in one country might play out completely differently in another. So, while the research identifies common themes and barriers across several cases, these should be seen as patterns, not universal laws.

Finally, a word about timing. The projects examined are relatively recent. That means the documents analysed in this research only capture a snapshot in time. Some of the barriers discussed might already have been overcome, while others could emerge later. A project that looked promising at the time of writing might stall tomorrow, or vice versa. This research can only speak to the situation as it stood when the data was collected.

All of that said, we still believe this work makes a valuable contribution. If nothing else, it sheds light on what often gets left out of the conversation, the messy, complicated, and sometimes disappointing reality of trying to bring blockchain into land registries. That doesn't mean the tech has no future here. But if future projects want to succeed, they'll need to look beyond the buzzwords and start addressing the real issues. We hope that our contribution will help to facilitate this process.

Bibliography

AARVIK, P. (2024). *Anti-corruption reforms have been successful in Georgia, but blockchain is stealing the limelight.* U4 Anti-Corruption Resource Centre. https://www.u4.no/blog/anti-corruption-reforms-successful-in-georgia-blockchain-stealing-limelight

AMEYAW, P. D. (2024). *Blockchain Technology for a Transparent Land Administration System: Feasibility Assessment for Adoption in Ghana's Land Sector* [Technische Universität München]. https://mediatum.ub.tum.de/603824?show_id=1747179&change_language=en

AMEYAW, P. D., & DE VRIES, W. T. (2021). Toward Smart Land Management: Land Acquisition and the Associated Challenges in Ghana. A Look into a Blockchain Digital Land Registry for Prospects. *Land, 10*(3), Article 3. https://doi.org/10.3390/land10030239

AMEYAW, P. D., & DE VRIES, W. T. (2023). Blockchain technology adaptation for land administration services: The importance of socio-cultural elements. *Land Use Policy, 125*, 106485. https://doi.org/10.1016/j.landusepol.2022.106485

ANSAH, B. O., VOSS, W., ASIAMA, K. O., & WUNI, I. Y. (2023). A systematic review of the institutional success factors for blockchain-based land administration. *Land Use Policy, 125*, 106473. https://doi.org/10.1016/j.landusepol.2022.106473

BAAKO, K. T., AFENYO, J. D., & GLOVER, V. (2022). *Barriers to the Adoption of Blockchain for Land Administration in a Developing Economy.* https://www.prres.org/uploads/548/2367/Baako_Barriers_Blockchain.pdf

BENNETT, R. M., UNGER, E.-M., LEMMEN, C., & DIJKSTRA, P. (2021). Land Administration Maintenance: A Review of the Persistent Problem and Emerging Fit-for-Purpose Solutions. *Land, 10*(5), Article 5. https://doi.org/10.3390/land10050509

BENNETT, R., MILLER, T., PICKERING, M., & KARA, A.-K. (2021). Hybrid Approaches for Smart Contracts in Land Administration: Lessons from Three Blockchain Proofs-of-Concept. *Land, 10*(2), Article 2. https://doi.org/10.3390/land10020220

BHATTACHARYA, A. (2018, 18). *Blockchain is helping build a new Indian city, but it's no cure for corruption.* Quartz. https://qz.com/india/1325423/indias-andhra-state-is-using-blockchain-to-build-capital-amaravati

P. L. Reiser et al., *Blockchain in Global Land Registries*,
https://doi.org/10.1007/978-3-658-50076-4

COLEMAN, L. (2016, April 7). Bitland Blockchain Initiative Seeks To Create Reliable Land Titles In Africa. *CCN.Com*. https://www.ccn.com/bitland-blockchain-initiative-seeks-to-create-reliable-land-titles-in-africa/

COMINCIOLI, L. M. (2021). *Can Blockchain Solve Corruption Problems in Land Administration in Developing Countries? – The Case of India* [Centre International De Formation Européenne Institut Européenne]. https://www.ie-ei.eu/Ressources/FCK/image/Theses/2021/Thesis_COMINCIOLI_GEGPA.pdf

DANG, D. A., DANG, K. K., DANG, V. A., & VU, T. L. (2020). The effects of trust and land administration on economic outcomes: Evidence from Vietnam. *Food Policy, 94*, 101813. https://doi.org/10.1016/j.foodpol.2019.101813

DANIEL, D., & IFEJIKA SPERANZA, C. (2020). The Role of Blockchain in Documenting Land Users' Rights: The Canonical Case of Farmers in the Vernacular Land Market. *Frontiers in Blockchain, 3*. https://doi.org/10.3389/fbloc.2020.00019

DJURSÉN, L., & BJÖRK, T. (2022). *Blockchain Adoption is an Evolution – not a Revolution:: Advantages and Challenges of Blockchain in Real Estate Transaction in Sweden.* https://urn.kb.se/resolve?urn=urn:nbn:se:kth:diva-314410

GARCIA-TERUEL, R. M. (2020). Legal challenges and opportunities of blockchain technology in the real estate sector. *Journal of Property, Planning and Environmental Law, 12*(2), 129–145. https://doi.org/10.1108/JPPEL-07-2019-0039

JANBANDHU, S., SAINDANE, D., JADHAV, R., GAWALE, P., & WAYKAR, S. (2023). Land Registration & Transfer of Entitlement using Blockchain. *International Journal for Research in Applied Science and Engineering Technology, 11*(3), 2044–2050. https://doi.org/10.22214/ijraset.2023.49885

JONATHAN, K. (2021). *Sweden Moves to Next Stage With Blockchain Land Registry*. CoinDesk. https://www.coindesk.com/markets/2017/03/30/sweden-moves-to-next-stage-with-blockchain-land-registry

JONSSON, J. R. (2018). *Perceived Affordance and Socio-Technical Transition: Blockchain for the Swedish Public Sector.* https://urn.kb.se/resolve?urn=urn:nbn:se:kth:diva-237533

JORGEN, M. (2021, February 8). *Balancing Blockchain and AI: ChromaWay and the Swedish Land Registry Submit Findings for Government Report* [Interview]. https://blog.chromia.com/balancing-blockchain-and-ai-chromaway-and-the-swedish-land-registry-submit-findings-for-government-report/

KACZOROWSKA, M. (2019). Blockchain-based Land Registration: Possibilities and Challenges. *Masaryk University Journal of Law and Technology, 13*(2), Article 2. https://doi.org/10.5817/MUJLT2019-2-8

KAPOOR, A., ESPOSITO, M., & ANAND, M. (2024). *Land Record Management in India* (SSRN Scholarly Paper No. 4811021). Social Science Research Network. https://doi.org/10.2139/ssrn.4811021

KAUSHIK, A. (2020). New technology interventions including blockchain technology in land record and registry management in India. *Proceedings of the 13th International*

Conference on Theory and Practice of Electronic Governance, 143–151. https://doi.org/10.1145/3428502.3428521

Križanović, J., Pivac, D., Tomić, H., & Mastelić-Ivić, S. (2021). Review of Land Administration Data Dissemination Practices: Case Study on Four Different Land Administration System Types. *Land, 10*(11), Article 11. https://doi.org/10.3390/land10111175

Kshetri, N. (2022). Blockchain as a tool to facilitate property rights protection in the Global South: Lessons from India's Andhra Pradesh state. *Third World Quarterly, 43*(2), 371–392. https://doi.org/10.1080/01436597.2021.2013116

Kumar, A., & Motwani, D. (2025). *The Applicability of Blockchain Technology in Land Registration for Developing Economies: A Case Study of India.* https://doi.org/10.13140/RG.2.2.21888.75520

Lazuashvili, N., Norta, A., & Draheim, D. (2019). Integration of Blockchain Technology into a Land Registration System for Immutable Traceability: A Casestudy of Georgia. In C. Di Ciccio, R. Gabryelczyk, L. García-Bañuelos, T. Hernaus, R. Hull, M. Indihar Štemberger, A. Kő, & M. Staples (Eds.), *Business Process Management: Blockchain and Central and Eastern Europe Forum* (pp. 219–233). Springer International Publishing. https://doi.org/10.1007/978-3-030-30429-4_15

Lemieux, V. L. (2016). Trusting records: Is Blockchain technology the answer? *Records Management Journal, 26*(2), 110–139. https://doi.org/10.1108/RMJ-12-2015-0042

Mansoor, M. A., Ali, M., Mateen, A., Kaleem, M., & Nazir, S. (2023). Blockchain Technology for Land Registry Management in Developing Countries. *2023 2nd International Conference on Emerging Trends in Electrical, Control, and Telecommunication Engineering (ETECTE)*, 1–6. https://doi.org/10.1109/ETECTE59617.2023.10396736

McMurren, J., Young, A., & Verhulst, S. (2018). *Addressing Transaction Costs Through Blockchain and Identity in Swedish Land Transfers.*

Mezquita, Y., Parra, J., Perez, E., Prieto, J., & Corchado, J. M. (2021). Blockchain-Based Systems in Land Registry, A Survey of Their Use and Economic Implications. In Á. Herrero, C. Cambra, D. Urda, J. Sedano, H. Quintián, & E. Corchado (Eds.), *13th International Conference on Computational Intelligence in Security for Information Systems (CISIS 2020)* (pp. 13–22). Springer International Publishing. https://doi.org/10.1007/978-3-030-57805-3_2

Miles, M. B., & Huberman, A. M. (1994). *Qualitative data analysis: An expanded sourcebook, 2nd ed* (2nd ed., pp. xiv, 338). Sage Publications, Inc. https://psycnet.apa.org/record/1995-97407-000

Miles, M. B., Huberman, A. M., & Saldaña, J. (2014). Qualitative Data Analysis: A Methods Sourcebook. Third Edition. In *SAGE Publications Ltd (CA).* SAGE Publications.

Müller, H., & Seifert, M. (2019). *Blockchain, a Feasible Technology for Land Administration?*

Olsen, B. L. (2018). *Beyond the Hype: Exploring Blockchain Technology in Land Administration* [Copenhagen Business School]. https://research-api.cbs.dk/ws/portalfiles/portal/59754431/576416_Masters_thesis_2018_66937_Final_1_.pdf

Proskurovska, A., & Dörry, S. (2022). The blockchain challenge for Sweden's housing and mortgage markets. *Environment and Planning A*, *54*(8), 1569–1585. https://doi.org/10.1177/0308518X221116896

Rodima-Taylor, D. (2021). Digitalizing land administration: The geographies and temporalities of infrastructural promise. *Geoforum*, *122*, 140–151. https://doi.org/10.1016/j.geoforum.2021.04.003

Saari, A., Vimpari, J., & Junnila, S. (2022). Blockchain in real estate: Recent developments and empirical applications. *Land Use Policy*, *121*, 106334. https://doi.org/10.1016/j.landusepol.2022.106334

Saldaña, J. (2021). *The Coding Manual for Qualitative Researchers* (4th ed.). SAGE Publications Ltd. https://collegepublishing.sagepub.com/products/the-coding-manual-for-qualitative-researchers-4-273583

Shang, Q., & Price, A. (2019). A Blockchain-Based Land Titling Project in the Republic of Georgia: Rebuilding Public Trust and Lessons for Future Pilot Projects. *Innovations: Technology, Governance, Globalization*, *12*(3–4), 72–78. https://doi.org/10.1162/inov_a_00276

Sharma, A., Gupta, R., Seth, J. K., & Garg, S. (2021). Blockchain and Government. In *Handbook of Green Computing and Blockchain Technologies* (1st ed.). CRC Press. https://doi.org/10.1201/9781003107507-9

Sharma, P., Nagariya, R., Kumar, M., & Patel, B. S. (2022). Analysis of the barriers of blockchain adoption in Land Record System. In *Industry 4.0 and Climate Change*. CRC Press.

Shuaib, M., Alam, S., Ahmed, R., Qamar, S., Nasir, M. S., & Alam, M. S. (2022). Current Status, Requirements, and Challenges of Blockchain Application in Land Registry. *International Journal of Information Retrieval Research (IJIRR)*, *12*(2), 1–20. https://doi.org/10.4018/IJIRR.299934

Tan, E., Mahula, S., & Crompvoets, J. (2022). Blockchain governance in the public sector: A conceptual framework for public management. *Government Information Quarterly*, *39*(1), 101625. https://doi.org/10.1016/j.giq.2021.101625

Teraji, S. (2008). Property rights, trust, and economic performance. *The Journal of Socio-Economics*, *37*(4), 1584–1596. https://doi.org/10.1016/j.socec.2007.06.008

Thakur, V., Doja, M. N., Dwivedi, Y. K., Ahmad, T., & Khadanga, G. (2020). Land records on Blockchain for implementation of Land Titling in India. *International Journal of Information Management*, *52*, 101940. https://doi.org/10.1016/j.ijinfomgt.2019.04.013

The Land Registry in the Blockchain. (2016). https://ica-it.org/pdf/Blockchain_Landregistry_Report.pdf

THOMAS, R. (2017). Blockchain's incompatibility for use as a land registry: Issues of definition, feasibility and risk. *European Property Law Journal, 6*(3), 361–390. https://doi.org/10.1515/eplj-2017-0021

TRIPATHI, G., AHAD, M. A., & CASALINO, G. (2023). A comprehensive review of blockchain technology: Underlying principles and historical background with future challenges. *Decision Analytics Journal, 9*, 100344. https://doi.org/10.1016/j.dajour.2023.100344

UN E-GOVERNMENT SURVEY 2024 (13th ed.). (2024). United Nations Department of Economic and Social Affairs. https://publicadministration.un.org/egovkb/en-us/Reports/UN-E-Government-Survey-2024

UN-ECE. (1996). *Land Administration Guidelines With Special Reference to Countries in Transition | UNECE.* https://unece.org/housing-and-land-management/publications/land-administration-guidelines-special-reference-countries

v. WEIZSÄCKER, F., EGGLER, S., & ATARIM, E. (2018, December 5). *Land registries on a distributed ledger.* Deutsche Gesellschaft für Internationale Zusammenarbeit (GIZ). https://www.giz.de/de/downloads/giz2019-en-distributed-land-registry.pdf

XIE, D., & XU, M. (2024). The Role of Trust in Facilitating Land Transfers and Contract Formalization: A Study of Chinese Farm Households. *Land, 13*(12), Article 12. https://doi.org/10.3390/land13122088

YAGA, D. J., MELL, P. M., ROBY, N., & SCARFONE, K. (2018). Blockchain Technology Overview. *NIST.* https://www.nist.gov/publications/blockchain-technology-overview

ZEIN, R. M., & TWINOMURINZI, H. (2023). Blockchain Technology in Lands Registration: A Systematic Literature Review. *JeDEM – eJournal of eDemocracy and Open Government, 15*(2), Article 2. https://doi.org/10.29379/jedem.v15i2.748

ZEVENBERGEN, J. (2004). A Systems Approach to Land Registration and Cadastre. *Nordic Journal of Surveying and Real Estate Research, 1*(1), Article 1. https://journal.fi/njs/article/view/41503

ZHENG, Z., XIE, S., DAI, H., CHEN, X., & WANG, H. (2017). An Overview of Blockchain Technology: Architecture, Consensus, and Future Trends. *2017 IEEE International Congress on Big Data (BigData Congress)*, 557–564. https://doi.org/10.1109/BigDataCongress.2017.85

Appendix

Appendix 1: **Table showing which first cycle codes are within the second cycle codes**

First Cycle – Descriptive Codes	Second Cycle – Thematic Codes
Lacking land data (mapping)	Data Quality and Record Issues
Trusted golden source for property data – success factor	Data Quality and Record Issues
Poor current record keeping	Data Quality and Record Issues
Data quality – no golden source	Data Quality and Record Issues
Lacking digitalization of LASs	Data Quality and Record Issues
Data consistency and quality	Data Quality and Record Issues
Lacking underlaying registry framework	Data Quality and Record Issues
Poor paper-based data	Data Quality and Record Issues
Unfinished Basic Digitalization	Data Quality and Record Issues
Quality of data	Data Quality and Record Issues
Certainty of Starting data	Data Quality and Record Issues
Data integrity potential for fraud	Data Quality and Record Issues
Data accuracy	Data Quality and Record Issues
Land Record Data Quality	Data Quality and Record Issues
Data Consistency	Data Quality and Record Issues
Problems with existing records	Data Quality and Record Issues
Poor quality of existing land records	Data Quality and Record Issues
Data quality – success factor	Data Quality and Record Issues
Digital Literacy	Education and Literacy
Private and Public Digital literacy – success factor	Education and Literacy
Understanding the tech for Trust	Education and Literacy
Limited BC knowledge	Education and Literacy
Understanding the Technology	Education and Literacy
Lack of Education about registries	Education and Literacy
Lack of digital literacy	Education and Literacy

P. L. Reiser et al., *Blockchain in Global Land Registries*,
https://doi.org/10.1007/978-3-658-50076-4

First Cycle – Descriptive Codes	Second Cycle – Thematic Codes
Government digital literacy	Education and Literacy
Educating Government	Education and Literacy
Lack of BC experts	Education and Literacy
Short supply of BC experts	Education and Literacy
Limited education possibilities	Education and Literacy
Decision makers BC education	Education and Literacy
Basic Literacy	Education and Literacy
Public and Private sector education	Education and Literacy
Limited tech awareness	Education and Literacy
Education – success factor	Education and Literacy
Changes in public sector	Governmental Power and Cooperation
Data governance among participating parties	Governmental Power and Cooperation
Institutional goal explorative in nature	Governmental Power and Cooperation
Institutional power resistance	Governmental Power and Cooperation
Government Loss of Power	Governmental Power and Cooperation
Importance of e-government – success factor	Governmental Power and Cooperation
Key Stakeholder buy-in	Governmental Power and Cooperation
Political barriers intervention from above	Governmental Power and Cooperation
Lack of political will	Governmental Power and Cooperation
Institutional Governance issues	Governmental Power and Cooperation
Ghana Government Cooperation	Governmental Power and Cooperation
Vital Public-private cooperation – success factor	Governmental Power and Cooperation
Community Support	Governmental Power and Cooperation
Cooperation unclear	Governmental Power and Cooperation
Government investment	Governmental Power and Cooperation
Political support of necessary change	Governmental Power and Cooperation
Regional vs. National Support	Governmental Power and Cooperation
Government Motivation	Governmental Power and Cooperation
Network limitations	Infrastructure Limitations
Internet Connectivity	Infrastructure Limitations
Stable electricity	Infrastructure Limitations
Inadequate Energy Infrastructure	Infrastructure Limitations
Poor electrical infrastructure	Infrastructure Limitations
Unstable Energy and internet connectivity	Infrastructure Limitations
Electricity and internet availability	Infrastructure Limitations
Internet Access	Infrastructure Limitations
Energy constraints	Infrastructure Limitations
Network infrastructure	Infrastructure Limitations

Appendix 1

First Cycle – Descriptive Codes	Second Cycle – Thematic Codes
Regulatory uncertainty	Legal and Regulatory Framework
Smart contract law	Legal and Regulatory Framework
Legal adaptations for blockchain	Legal and Regulatory Framework
Digital signatures legal challenge	Legal and Regulatory Framework
Legal validity of BC contracts	Legal and Regulatory Framework
Progress once digital signatures accepted	Legal and Regulatory Framework
Legal recognition of digital processes	Legal and Regulatory Framework
Law and practice differences	Legal and Regulatory Framework
Blockchain legal framework necessary	Legal and Regulatory Framework
Further legislative research	Legal and Regulatory Framework
Institutional legal support	Legal and Regulatory Framework
Legal validity of digital titles	Legal and Regulatory Framework
Legal Validity of Electronic signatures	Legal and Regulatory Framework
Regulation update	Legal and Regulatory Framework
Legal Issues with current ownership system	Legal and Regulatory Framework
Understanding & Enforcement of Digital Signatures	Legal and Regulatory Framework
Legal validity	Legal and Regulatory Framework
Legislative framework regarding data – success factor	Legal and Regulatory Framework
Unresolved ownership disputes	Legal and Regulatory Framework
Legal limitations smart contracts	Legal and Regulatory Framework
Lack of legal enforcement for land registry	Legal and Regulatory Framework
Inefficient enforcement of law	Legal and Regulatory Framework
Legal uncertainty in data sharing	Legal and Regulatory Framework
Officials concerned with transparency	Preservation of Status Quo
Transparency not welcome	Preservation of Status Quo
Resistance to transparency	Preservation of Status Quo
No Incentive to adopt change	Preservation of Status Quo
Preference for privacy of ownership	Preservation of Status Quo
Preference for physical transactions	Preservation of Status Quo
Legacy system complications	Technical Limitations
Functionality of smart contracts	Technical Limitations
Legacy System Limitations	Technical Limitations
Lack of blockchain maturity	Technical Limitations
Does not solve centralization	Technical Limitations
Identity Verification	Technical Limitations
Scalability issues	Technical Limitations
Technical limitations smart contracts	Technical Limitations
Clarity about Smart contracts	Technical Limitations

First Cycle – Descriptive Codes	Second Cycle – Thematic Codes
Mistrust from regulatory uncertainty	Trust and Perception
Public perception / trust in institutions	Trust and Perception
Public distrust of system	Trust and Perception
Public mistrust of government	Trust and Perception
Mistrust in technology	Trust and Perception
Lack of trust in digital contracts	Trust and Perception
Distrust of government intentions	Trust and Perception
Mistrust in current system	Trust and Perception
Landowners mistrust of people in charge of BC	Trust and Perception
Mistrust of technology	Trust and Perception

Appendix 2: Table showing direct quotations from the analyzed sources

ISO	Source	Descriptive Code	Thematic Code	Segment
SE	Jonsson, 2018	Decision makers BC education	Education and Literacy	The first recommendation is to actively educate developers and decision makers about the technology.
SE	Jonathan, 2021	Institutional goal explorative in nature	Government, Control and Cooperation	SBAB Bank however said it has no immediate plans to implement the tech, saying: "Our reason to participate in the project has not been to actually implement the solution in our current processes. But rather an opportunity for us to get a better understanding of the blockchain technology and how it might possibly fit in our future products/offerings.
SE	Jonsson, 2018	Changes in public sector	Government, Control and Cooperation	This section presents the answers to the research question: 'What actions are needed from the public sector to enable leveraging on blockchain?' by including the recommended actions and considerations to the Swedish public sector, which are argued to be beneficial or necessary for the future adoption of blockchain.
SE	McMurren et al., 2018	Data governance among participating parties	Government, Control and Cooperation	Frameworks for data governance and the incorporation of these parties must still be defined. Thus, scalability remains a challenge.
SE	Proskurovska & Dörry, 2022	Institutional power resistance	Government, Control and Cooperation	Interviewees Proskurovska and Dörry suggested that Lantmäteriet – currently the sole authority of Sweden's land registries – would need to cede control, but 'then the banks would also become a part of [the system] (...) And to do that we have to change the way we work together'.
SE	Proskurovska & Dörry, 2022	Institutional power resistance	Government, Control and Cooperation	While under the current arrangements the scale-up of the application is nearly impossible, solutions are being worked on
SE	Proskurovska & Dörry, 2022	Institutional power resistance	Government, Control and Cooperation	From an institutional perspective, the described power struggle between vested private interests to resist, defend and admittedly arbitrage the current system on the one hand, and a more transparent – public – governance information system crucial to improving the shortcomings of the current housing sales system linked to fiscal and monetary spaces and risks, may point to strong resistance against change
SE	Shuaib et al., 2022	Data governance among participating parties	Government, Control and Cooperation	framework for data governance for the involved stakeholder in the process. (scalability)
SE	R. Bennett et al., 2021	Data governance among participating parties	Government, Control and Cooperation	This large number of stakeholders would draw a massive amount of data and bandwidth resources. Therefore, data governance problems and scalability need to be resolved
SE	R. Bennett et al., 2021	Digital signatures legal challenge	Legal and Regulatory Framework	A major challenge identified during the proof-of-concept assessment is that Swedish law does not allow for the use of electronic signatures for property transactions, obviously a major constraint in terms of scaling the project to production level.

ISO	Source	Descriptive Code	Thematic Code	Segment
SE	R. Bennett et al., 2021	Progress once digital signatures accepted	Legal and Regulatory Framework	In terms of current status, the blockchain network and smart contract proof-of-concept protocol were trialled and externally tested. Further progress can start once the digital signature restrictions are addressed.
SE	Djursén & Björk, 2022	Legal validity of BC contracts	Legal and Regulatory Framework	The second concern was the legal recognition of blockchain based contracts, with the relevant contracts still needing to be put into an EU standard format before being examined independently.
SE	Jonathan, 2021	Digital signatures legal challenge	Legal and Regulatory Framework	"We want to work fully digitally, but the law requires, at the moment, physical signatures on the papers, which makes it difficult," explained Kempe.
SE	Jonsson, 2018	Regulation update	Legal and Regulatory Framework	The third recommendation is the revision of regulations. For the public sector to be able to fully leverage on blockchain, regulations need to be updated to suit the modern digital era. It is important that regulations are kept technology-neutral to not restrict development.
SE	Jorgen, 2021	Digital signatures legal challenge	Legal and Regulatory Framework	Currently, the project is pending new legislation by the government. A sticking point in Sweden is that you need a paper signature for property transfers.
SE	Jorgen, 2021	Digital signatures legal challenge	Legal and Regulatory Framework	They have a phrasing that a digital signature should be equivalent to a paper signature, but real estate transactions are actually exempt from this rule.
SE	McMurren et al., 2018	Digital signatures legal challenge	Legal and Regulatory Framework	The principal legal concern for moving the pilot toward broader implementation relates to uncertainty about the validity of digital signatures for real estate contracts.
SE	McMurren et al., 2018	Digital signatures legal challenge	Legal and Regulatory Framework	Historically, Swedish law required a physical signature on real estate contracts, and although both Swedish and European law are increasingly allowing electronic identification, the legal status of digital signatures for real estate has not been established in court.
SE	Müller & Seifert, 2019	Digital signatures legal challenge	Legal and Regulatory Framework	A legal feature in Sweden, which stipulates that signatures on a physical paper must be provided in real estate transactions, has proven to be problematic.
SE	Proskurovska & Dörry, 2022	Legal uncertainty in data sharing	Legal and Regulatory Framework	One obstacle is the current lack of a legal framework that would enable the seamless sharing of public data between public actors, as well as their reliance on automated processes.
SE	Proskurovska & Dörry, 2022	Digital signatures legal challenge	Legal and Regulatory Framework	A popular explanation is the missing legislation that would make digitally signed DS equivalent to hand-signed paper DS
SE	Proskurovska & Dörry, 2022	Digital signatures legal challenge	Legal and Regulatory Framework	Moreover, as legislation to recognise digital signatures for real estate transactions is on hold, we can conclude that, for the time being, the incumbent institutions will not only remain largely unchallenged.
SE	Shuaib et al., 2022	Digital signatures legal challenge	Legal and Regulatory Framework	Legal validity of digital signature for land registry contract

Appendix 2

ISO	Source	Descriptive Code	Thematic Code	Segment
SE	Djursén & Björk, 2022	No Incentive to adopt change	Preservation of Status Quo	Another challenge found in the interview with Renström is that information asymmetry in a transaction can be beneficial for an experienced buyer or seller. The reason is that those opportunities and risks can come from information asymmetry, which would mean that some actors in the market would be reluctant to adopt the technology. Since they otherwise could capitalize on the information asymmetry.
SE	Djursén & Björk, 2022	Identity Verification	Technical Limitations	The first roadblock involved issues with identity verification, with the presentation demonstrating the use of current centralized technology to validate signatures along the transaction chain
SE	Garcia-Teruel, 2020	Functionality of smart contracts	Technical Limitations	Current projects, which focus on blockchain and the use of smart contracts, allow the owner to sell the property while this transaction is registered at the same time. This is the case of the Landmateriet in Sweden and other projects from private initiatives such as Velow.re. However, the range of rights that can created and registered in land registers is wider in practice. It might be difficult to translate certain rights into the code of a smart contract, both rights in rem and even the clauses of a tenancy contract.
SE	McMurren et al., 2018	Legacy System Limitations	Technical Limitations	In addition, security provisions built into legacy systems have prevented further digitization of the land transfer process, for example by imposing restrictions through firewalls and limits on network connections. As a result, while some institutional actors (including realtors, banks, and some government agencies) could connect their systems to Lantmäteriet databases, individual buyers and sellers could not.
SE	Djursén & Björk, 2022	Mistrust from regulatory uncertainty	Trust and Perception	a large percentage has a great concern regarding regulatory uncertainty and a lack of trust among users
SE	Jonathan, 2021	Lack of trust in digital contracts	Trust and Perception	While trust in digital contracts has been lagging for a long time, he argued that blockchain tech can now provide the trust needed to move forward. “As soon as the legislator understands that this is possible, I think it will come true,” said Kempe.
IN	Bhattacharya, 2018	Quality of data	Data Quality and Record Issues	“Whatever data we are trying to (put on the) blockchain, the data need to be purified. As a department, your responsibility is to make sure you are digitising the correct record,” admitted CRDA commissioner Sreedhar.
IN	Comincioli, 2021	Certainty of Starting data	Data Quality and Record Issues	A land-record system based on Blockchain request a high degree of certainty, the data uploaded on the blockchain cannot contain wrong information, neither they can contain transactions with disputes still pending, the problem in developing countries such as India, is that data regarding land properties and those regarding purchase and sale transactions present a certain frequency show discrepancy, this problem must be resolved before the blockchain is being implemented, if not the information uploaded will prove to be wrong

ISO	Source	Descriptive Code	Thematic Code	Segment
IN	Kapoor et al., 2024	Data integrity potential for fraud	Data Quality and Record Issues	A modification in one title necessitates adjustments in other titles, creating a cascade of modifications in the RoRs. This, in turn, raises the issue of potential data tampering before the data is put on a DLT-based land record management platform.
IN	Kapoor et al., 2024	Data accuracy	Data Quality and Record Issues	The key challenge remains one of ensuring real-time accuracy, that is, up-to-date land records, accessible to the common citizen, beyond mere formalities of computerisation and digitisation.
IN	Kshetri, 2022	Land Record Data Quality	Data Quality and Record Issues	Second, while blockchain systems are secure and trustworthy, their data – like that of other databases – are only as accurate as what is entered. In AP's case, some of the land records are reported to be of poor quality. Without clean records, blockchain's potential as a trust machine cannot be realised.
IN	Kshetri, 2022	Data Consistency	Data Quality and Record Issues	A major barrier is that different systems from which data need to be transferred to the blockchain system use different data formats and models. The integration of diverse data and systems into blockchain platforms could be costly and time consuming.
IN	A. Sharma et al., 2021	Problems with existing records	Data Quality and Record Issues	This involves issues such as land data not being properly recorded in files, poor coordination among various departments resulting in delay in implementation, natural calamities cause lossing of documents, or disputes of ownership on land records.
IN	P. Sharma et al., 2022	Poor quality of existing land records	Data Quality and Record Issues	Due to the existence of poor quality land records, the introduction of blockchain to all land parcels is unsuitable.
IN	Comincioli, 2021	Lack of BC experts	Education and Literacy	a lack of experts specialized in the implementation of blockchain's architectures, the experts familiar with the different types (private, public, hybrid) of blockchains were and are still limited.
IN	Comincioli, 2021	Limited education possibilities	Education and Literacy	A limited number of governmental and private organizations whit the requested prerequisites to work and carry-out a successful training for public employees and administrators.
IN	Kshetri, 2022	Basic Literacy	Education and Literacy	Third, despite improving literacy rates in the state, a large proportion of the population lacks the literacy and digital skills required to benefit from the blockchain system. For instance, in 2020, AP's adult literacy rates were 80 % for males and 69 % for females.
IN	Kumar & Motwani, 2025	Public and Private sector education	Education and Literacy	Education and Training: Education and training of key government officials and other people involved in the process are necessary for a successful use of the blockchain technology in the land registry. This means that they have to be theoretical concerns about the technology, its benefits and how its limitations could be addressed.
IN	A. Sharma et al., 2021	Limited tech awareness	Education and Literacy	As blockchain is an emerging technology, there is a lack of awareness about the technology

Appendix 2

ISO	Source	Descriptive Code	Thematic Code	Segment
IN	A. Sharma et al., 2021	Short supply of BC experts	Education and Literacy	Even the implementing departments may face human resource constraints while working on this technology. At present the numbers of blockchain developers are meager in the world. The requisite experts of blockchain technology are in short supply, at least in India.
IN	Comincioli, 2021	Government investment	Government, Control and Cooperation	The cost of initially set-up a large network for the application of Blockchain is significant, many resources are required, and public investments are crucial.
IN	Kshetri, 2022	Political support of necessary change	Government, Control and Cooperation	the uptake and use of new technologies hinge critically on intention, desire and commitment on the part of a government to carry through significant political reforms as well as the agreement of and support from state officials and other key actors.
IN	Kshetri, 2022	Regional vs. National Support	Government, Control and Cooperation	despite the above-mentioned progress on the regulatory front in AP, some national-level regulations have posed a challenge. In 2018, India's central bank, the Reserve Bank of India (RBI), initiated a crackdown on cryptocurrencies. All RBI-regulated bodies were prohibited from having business relationships with entities dealing with cryptocurrencies, which negatively affected the blockchain ecosystem.
IN	Kshetri, 2022	Government Motivation	Government, Control and Cooperation	an inefficient bureaucracy has hampered the development and implementation of blockchain systems. As of August 2018, most blockchain projects in the AP had just completed the proof-of-concept (PoC) phase or were developing PoCs. Some government departments were not motivated to move beyond the PoC stage. There are also potential issues related to conflict and power relationships. In India, there has also been confusion regarding the central authority to handle blockchain systems.
IN	A. Sharma et al., 2021	Cooperation unclear	Government, Control and Cooperation	Various agencies are involved in land registries such as Estate and sub registrar ofices; hence, many cumbersome pre-processes need to be completed to make a synchronous system.
IN	Comincioli, 2021	Network limitations	Infrastructure Limitations	The set-up of a network with enough bandwidth to keep the nodes running is not simple. The availability of networks in India is still quite low.
IN	Kshetri, 2022	Internet Access	Infrastructure Limitations	a large proportion of the state's population lacks Internet access. As of January 2021, AP's Internet penetration was 31 %, which was below the national average of 36 %
IN	Kumar & Motwani, 2025	Energy constraints	Infrastructure Limitations	Energy Consumption: Such blockchains such as Bitcoin consume a lot of energy resulting from their consensus methods such as Proof of Work
IN	P. Sharma et al., 2022	Network infrastructure	Infrastructure Limitations	Considering the scale-up at the state or national level,the central cloud servers become an issue and thus may be a great failure point that can distort the total network.
IN	Comincioli, 2021	Legal Validity of Electronic signatures	Legal and Regulatory Framework	There are still problems deriving from the legislative systems, India and other countries have laws that prohibit the use of digital signatures or that do not take them into consideration for official documents,

ISO	Source	Descriptive Code	Thematic Code	Segment
IN	Comincioli, 2021	Regulatory uncertainty	Legal and Regulatory Framework	there is no regulation on how the transactions should be written and which is the minimum set of attributes needed for recording a transaction, rules should be fixed by a regulatory body, but it's still not clear which body should do that (at least in India).
IN	Kapoor et al., 2024	Legal Issues with current ownership system	Legal and Regulatory Framework	In India, the legal framework is centred around registered sale deeds rather than land titles. The Transfer of Property Act of 1882 mandates transferring or selling the right to immovable property through registered documents governed by the Registration Act of 1908. Consequently, transactions are registered, not the land title itself, creating a situation where ownership is not always guaranteed, and previous transactions may face challenges. Moreover, certain property transactions are not mandatory to register under the Registration Act, leading to unrecorded divisions and potential disputes over property ownership.
IN	Kshetri, 2022	Smart Contract Law	Legal and Regulatory Framework	The lack of blockchain standards and legal and regulatory frameworks for smart contracts has also been of concern. In smart contracts, computerised protocols and user interfaces are used to execute a contract's terms and to 'formalize and secure relationships over public networks'. AP's blockchain system uses smart contracts to allow instant data exchange with banks and financial institutions. This feature makes it possible for landowners to access loan and financial services efficiently. However, there are no clear regulations regarding smart contracts in India.
IN	Kshetri, 2022	Understanding & Enforcement of Digital Signatures	Legal and Regulatory Framework	Regulatory and enforcement issues related to public key infrastructure (PKI) and underdeveloped privacy and security practices are not well developed. For instance, while India's Information Technology Act 2000 provides the legal basis for e-signatures, there is a low level of understanding of digital signature laws. Some may thus be concerned about the legal aspects of blockchain-based land records.
IN	Kumar & Motwani, 2025	Legal validity	Legal and Regulatory Framework	To have the records of land ownership on the blockchain open to the use of the public as it eases verification a crucial step is getting the various governments in the world to pass laws as to allow electronic certificates to be used as proof of land ownership.
IN	A. Sharma et al., 2021	Unresolved ownership disputes	Legal and Regulatory Framework	A very large number of disputes have been registered in courts regarding land issues, such as ownership con"icts, title of the properties, cost of the properties. There are many judicial and administrative forums where such unresolved cases are pending. Those needing resolution before getting transferred to blockchain may take more than 10 years to resolve.
IN	Bhattacharya, 2018	Does not solve centralization	Technical Limitations	This addition of a middle-man can throw a spanner in the works even for a relatively hack-proof technology like blockchain. "Land registries generally speaking won't make too much sense if you still

Appendix 2

ISO	Source	Descriptive Code	Thematic Code	Segment
IN	Bhattacharya, 2018	Does not solve centralization	Technical Limitations	(continued from page 88) have a government office in the middle which you need to trust in order to transfer property," said Markos Zachariadis, associate professor at Warwick Business School and a fintech research fellow at the University of Cambridge. Of course, it helps if a record is lost or tampered with, or damaged in a natural disaster. But it does little to curb manipulation by those in charge of the data being transferred to the blockchain.
IN	Kaushik, 2020	Clarity about Smart contracts	Technical Limitations	However, a tremendous degree of coordination and clarity on how smart contracts are designed, verified, implemented and enforced will be required.
IN	Kshetri, 2022	Legacy System Complications	Technical Limitations	Finally, the experiences of government blockchain projects in AP and other Indian states have shown that the migration and integration of legacy IT and database management systems into a blockchain-based system would be a difficult task. A major barrier is that different systems from which data need to be transferred to the blockchain system use different data formats and models. The integration of diverse data and systems into blockchain platforms could be costly and time consuming.
IN	Kumar & Motwani, 2025	Scalability issues	Technical Limitations	Scalability: Solana has a great throughput too bad other blockchains like Ethereum still have to deal with their scaling person once more transactions per time comes into play.
IN	Bhattacharya, 2018	Public mistrust of government	Trust and Perception	Having seen the government's dirty tricks, most of the farmers gathered at Rayapudi aren't buying the claim that the system is tamper-proof – especially at the stages before the information is moved to blockchain. After all, assignments and verifications are still being done by revenue officers on the ground.
IN	Bhattacharya, 2018	Public distrust of system	Trust and Perception	That the Andhra Pradesh government is using a private blockchain complicates things further. The public can view information but not directly monitor whether any illicit changes have been made to their records. They have to go through the usual red tape to get those answers. The system may not be susceptible to hacking, but authorities could deliberately enter wrong information or refuse to reveal instances of fraud even if they are logged. This is the farmers' biggest concern.
IN	Bhattacharya, 2018	Public mistrust of government	Trust and Perception	"The tampering cannot be stopped. If you give the right people a lot of bribe, they will go in and change the record," said Seshagiri Rao. Nearly $700 million is paid in bribes across land registrars in India, an Andhra Pradesh government official estimated last year, and even probes into these matters are often flawed.
IN	Bhattacharya, 2018	Public mistrust of government	Trust and Perception	But landowners have little faith in a system that relies on the government to put its own safeguards in place. In fact, even farmers who have allowed their land to be pooled, registered their plots, and accessed the maps online feel left in the dark

ISO	Source	Descriptive Code	Thematic Code	Segment
IN	Comincioli, 2021	Mistrust in technology	Trust and Perception	The immutable nature of blockchain creates a sense of fear and distrust in the minds of employees and functionaries that will tend to continue to use existing computerized systems.
IN	Comincioli, 2021	Mistrust in current system	Trust and Perception	In most of States, citizens have little faith in the existing systems. Even if they have a valid sale deed, citizens are confused if they legally own a piece of land. Others who wish to acquire land are unsure whether the seller is the legitimate owner.
IN	Kapoor et al., 2024	Distrust of government intentions	Trust and Perception	Additionally, most tribal communities lack digital literacy, leading to widespread ignorance about digital procedures. Their recurring concern is that the digitisation program is a government attempt to take over tribal land for industrial use.
IN	Kaushik, 2020	Landowners mistrust of people in charge of BC	Trust and Perception	The land owners still have a fear of manipulation of records by those in charge of the data being transferred to the blockchain.
IN	P. Sharma et al., 2022	Mistrust of technology	Trust and Perception	Despite the much-hailed advantages of blockchain, many participants are afraid of dependency on blockchain operators
IN	Aarvik, 2024	Public perception / trust in institutions	Trust and Perception	The land registry in Andhra Pradesh, India, for example, struggles to ensure that information entered on the blockchain is correct. Unless the data-entry process is free from corruption, blockchain technology alone can't guarantee a trustworthy ledger.
GH	Ameyaw, 2024	Poor current record keeping	Data Quality and Record Issues	Poor and paper-based recordkeeping system
GH	Baako et al., 2022	Data quality – no golden source	Data Quality and Record Issues	"The technology is not plug-and-play. We have off chain issues (referring to issues that take place outside the technology) in Ghana, the main one is accuracy of data in the Lands administration sector. Ghana does not have authoritative property market data. The market is somewhat a jungle, and we are operating with silos of information. There is no central knowledge, no form of monitoring and people are just being ripped off their properties" (Blockchain Consultant).
GH	Baako et al., 2022	Lacking land data (mapping)	Data Quality and Record Issues	The analysis discovered barriers relating to the integrity of land sector data which would ultimately serve as a primary data source for digital technology. Majority of the respondents laid emphasis on historical and prevailing surveying and mapping challenges, which further exacerbate long-standing land disputes nationwide.
GH	Baako et al., 2022	Lacking digitalization of LASs	Data Quality and Record Issues	The analysis further highlighted incomplete coverage of registration and digitalisation in the country. The Ghana Enterprise Land Information System (GELIS), which represents Ghana's prevailing effort towards digitalisation, covers circa 10 % of all land data in the country.
GH	Coleman, 2016	Data consistency and quality	Data Quality and Record Issues	As Bitland works to transfer paper data into a digital format, it must also consolidate new land registry requests against the old registries, according to the

Appendix 2

ISO	Source	Descriptive Code	Thematic Code	Segment
GH	Coleman, 2016	Data consistency and quality	Data Quality and Record Issues	(continued from page 90) documents are outdated, and locals have their own ways to track titles. These problems must be solved to get a single registry that represents a consistent ledger of land title holdings.
GH	Coleman, 2016	Lacking underlaying registry framework	Data Quality and Record Issues	Ghana has had a Land Administration Project for 17 years to address land disputes. However, nepotism and corruption have undermined the project. The project has not been able to consolidate the land tracking title program
GH	Olsen, 2018	Unfinished Basic Digitalization	Data Quality and Record Issues	Digitalization of records and orthophoto-mapping of the entire country has not been completed.
GH	Olsen, 2018	Poor paper based data	Data Quality and Record Issues	Registry documents are still held locally and in paper-form and is unorganized, uncategorized and in poor physical shape
GH	Olsen, 2018	Unfinished Basic Digitalization	Data Quality and Record Issues	Orthophoto mapping and the lack of digitalization is also a structural problem that blockchain alone cannotsolve
GH	Olsen, 2018	Unfinished Basic Digitalization	Data Quality and Record Issues	Finally, the lack of digitization stands as a dire reminder of why BCT should be evaluated on practical considerations and discussed in the context of the environment. The paper-based system is a major impediment for introducing a blockchain system and might indicate that the technology has been introduced too early as the instrument for breaking the poverty cycle in Sub Saharan Africa.
GH	Ameyaw, 2024	Limited BC knowledge	Education and Literacy	Limited knowledge of officials in Blockchain
GH	Ameyaw & de Vries, 2023	Understanding the Technology	Education and Literacy	Public-stakeholder acceptance is however dependent on their awareness, and understanding of the technology.
GH	Baako et al., 2022	Lack of Education about registries	Education and Literacy	There are also several misconceptions associated with land registration in general in Ghana which will translate to BCT. Many Ghanaians, per our interviews, do not use title registration because they think it is reserved for the elite. The analysis shows that many middle-class real estate transacting parties do not see the usefulness of land registration, except as a way in which highly educated and "bookish" individuals flaunt their property ownership status. Not wanting to associate with this kind of perception, the former group desists from land registration, affecting land registration uptake.
GH	Baako et al., 2022	Lack of digital literacy	Education and Literacy	Finally, the analysis yielded low levels of digital literacy as a potential barrier to the adoption of BCT in Ghana. This is consistent with findings by Ehwi and Asante (2016) that land sector professionals need to upgrade their digital literacy if any digitisation efforts will see significant success. The following interview quote captures it perfectly.
GH	Olsen, 2018	Government digital literacy	Education and Literacy	Explaining Land Layby Listings to the government officials
GH	Olsen, 2018	Educating Government	Education and Literacy	Educating, convincing and highlighting the importance for rural communities to register property

ISO	Source	Descriptive Code	Thematic Code	Segment
GH	Ameyaw & de Vries, 2023	Key Stakeholder buy-in	Government, Control and Cooperation	Important is the recognition of customary land governance, and authority in a blockchain adaptation especially in countries with customary land tenure system. As noted earlier, customary tenure holds 80 % of all land in Ghana. Land administration system in Ghana can therefore not be complete without a good cooperation from customary landowners, especially the traditional authorities who act as custodians of customary lands. These traditional chiefs wield so much power, and control over the management and administration of customary lands although the Commission exercises supervisory role over these power, especially the power of disposition as stipulated under Article 267(3) of Ghana's constitution.
GH	Baako et al., 2022	Lack of political will	Government, Control and Cooperation	A critical analysis of the interviews revealed that directives implemented by the Lands Commission are not exempt from the influence of the executive arm of government, which is formed, and often dominated, by the political party in power. Essentially, the adoption or non-adoption of emerging technologies, such as Blockchain, for land administration in Ghana could be heavily impacted by the agenda of the government of the day, summed up in the concept of 'political will'. Where the political party that heads the government does not consider digitisation to be one of its priorities, the Lands Commission and other key sector agencies accordingly take a similar position.
GH	Baako et al., 2022	Political barriers intervention from above	Government, Control and Cooperation	In effect, for Blockchain technology to be adopted over the long term, the political barriers must be surmounted. Cooperation on the adoption and use of disruptive technologies such as Blockchain in Ghana's public land administration system typically lasts for as long as any political regime may accommodate. Similar studies by Khasawneh-Jalghoum and Wood-Harper (2011) recognise the existence of political barriers to the adoption of new technology
GH	Coleman, 2016	Institutional Governance issues	Government, Control and Cooperation	Ghana has had a Land Administration Project for 17 years to address land disputes. However, nepotism and corruption have undermined the project. The project has not been able to consolidate the land tracking title program.
GH	Olsen, 2018	Community Support	Government, Control and Cooperation	Achieving support from the community and trying to establish mutual cooperation with the government was also mentioned as problematic.
GH	Olsen, 2018	Ghana Government Cooperation	Government, Control and Cooperation	An interesting finding was the fact that none of the two companies interviewed was actively coordinating work or had a partnership with the Ghanaian government; they both worked independently with the communities in rural Ghana.
GH	Olsen, 2018	Ghana Government Cooperation	Government, Control and Cooperation	The consequences of missing coordination with authorities is also evidenced in past land registry projects. between 2007–2009 a consortium of companies led by Corporate Initiatives Development Group (CIDG) began documenting land rights of rural poor Ghanaians through a process they named

Appendix 2

ISO	Source	Descriptive Code	Thematic Code	Segment
GH	Olsen, 2018	Ghana Government Cooperation	Government, Control and Cooperation	(continued from page 92) the 'paralegal titling' project (Rabley, Aboah, Deroy, & Edmead, 2008). The assumption for the project was that the paralegal titles they registered would later become formalized (i.e. recognized) under the Lands Commission. In collaboration with Trimble Navigation and ESRI/ Sambus Ltd. they began using low-cost GIS software to capture satellite images and aerial photo documentation of the to-be registered land. The formalization through the Lands Commission did however never happen, and the project defaulted two years later (Jones-Casey & Knox, Ghana's Land Administration at a Crossroads, 2011)
GH	Zein & Twinomurinzi, 2023	Government Loss of Power	Government, Control and Cooperation	However, this also presents challenges. BT poses a significant threat to established power structures within governments.
GH	Ameyaw & de Vries, 2023	Stable electricity	Infrastructure Limitations	Thus, avenues for a stable electricity power support are an important consideration for blockchain adoption.
GH	Baako et al., 2022	Inadequate Energy Infrastructure	Infrastructure Limitations	A dominant concern raised by all respondents to the study was one of inadequate infrastructure to support the use of the technology. Erratic power supply coupled with limited cyber infrastructure and usage across the country featured significantly in the interview data. Respondents posited that unreliable power supply significantly disrupted economic activity hence the fortunes of Blockchain technology adoption remain similarly bleak.
GH	Coleman, 2016	Poor electrical infrastructure	Infrastructure Limitations	Bitland cannot, however, rely on existing local infrastructure solely on account of "rolling blackouts," a big problem in Ghana. The infrastructure is unreliable in many areas. There are 24- to 48-hour periods where large areas go without electricity. Hence, electronic solutions would not be feasible unless there were a failsafe as part of the ecosystem.
GH	Olsen, 2018	Unstable Energy and internet connectivity	Infrastructure Limitations	Electricity outages and Wi-fi connections
GH	Olsen, 2018	Electricity and internet availability	Infrastructure Limitations	When asked about key considerations of operating a blockchain registry in Ghana, electricity and internet access was problematic issues for Bitland at this point.
GH	Baako et al., 2022	Legal recognition of digital processes	Legal and Regulatory Framework	a prominent feature of Ghana's land sector is the manual or paper-based approach to land transaction processes. As a result, these practices have been preserved in law much to the detriment of digital interventions. Such lack of recognition further enshrines manual processes along with their associated challenges.
GH	Baako et al., 2022	Law and practice differences	Legal and Regulatory Framework	Indeed, the new Land Act, 2020 (Act 1036) makes provision for conveyancing by legal practitioners of land interests via an electronic information system; however, increased emphasis is still placed on paper-based transactions.

ISO	Source	Descriptive Code	Thematic Code	Segment
GH	Baako et al., 2022	Inefficient enforcement of law	Legal and Regulatory Framework	Respondents were of the view that the success or otherwise of Blockchain technology, even if adopted, depended largely on the pace of justice delivery amidst an ever-increasing backlog of land disputes and litigations.
GH	Olsen, 2018	Legal validity of digital titles	Legal and Regulatory Framework	The validity of the land records would most likely be questioned, at least in statutory courts, since the title has not been registered through the formal government channel and further has not been handled by formal surveyors from the Lands Commission or the CLS. Legitimacy in the registration process in regard to conformity of formal rules for land registration is therefore debatable since neither have involved formal surveyors from the government.
GH	Olsen, 2018	Lack of legal enforcement for land registry	Legal and Regulatory Framework	However, entitlement have little value if the policy is not backed by legal enforcement and active governance over the registry process in peri-urban and rural areas. Implementing a title system will likely help reduce multiple sales of land as it will be determined and registered who is the true owner or leaseholder of the disputed land.
GH	Ameyaw, 2024	Resistance to transparency	Preservation of Status Quo	Possibility of chiefs, as well as some public land sector officials, to undermine any system that will try to make their activities more transparent and accountable
GH	Ameyaw & de Vries, 2021	Officials concerned with transparency	Preservation of Status Quo	It is essential to mention that threats of system sabotage from some corrupt land officials, and customary authorities who might not wish for transparency in their deals, exist.
GH	Baako et al., 2022	Preference for physical transactions	Preservation of Status Quo	The interviewees revealed that most of their clients, educated and uneducated alike, are often not comfortable with signing of digital contracts for real estate transactions. Transacting parties are used to the presence of witnesses and the signing of physical documentation, and as such any technology that reduces this step be regarded as unsafe. Safety is of particular concern because of the huge funds usually involved in property transactions. The following quotes demonstrates thus barrier.
GH	Baako et al., 2022	Preference for privacy of ownership	Preservation of Status Quo	Another potential barrier to the adoption of BCT, and other technologies, in Ghana is the socio-cultural barrier of information hoarding. Generally, Ghanaians are very private with their information and avoid sharing information about property transactions. People simply do not want others to know about their ownership. The risk, perceived or real, of technology making public transactional data may dissuade Ghanaians from adopting the technology. This information "hoarding" persists despite the benefits of data transparency. This high level of sensitivity and anonymity that users in Ghana attach to real estate transactions has been captured in previous studies including Baako (2019).
GE	Shang & Price, 2019	Data quality – success factor	Data Quality and Record Issues	The success of the Georgia project was the result of two crucial elements – education and data quality.

Appendix 2

ISO	Source	Descriptive Code	Thematic Code	Segment
GE	Shang & Price, 2019	Data quality – success factor	Data Quality and Record Issues	More importantly, the existence of high-quality data helped guarantee the validity of the project. Without accurate data, the power of a Blockchain-based solution for a land registry would have been greatly limited, as poor-quality information posted on the Blockchain would make third-party verification of land titles difficult.
GE	v. Weizsäcker et al., 2018	Private and Public Digital literacy – success factor	Education and Literacy	Lastly, digital infrastructure and literacy are prerequirements for implementing a blockchain-based land registry system. This applies to both authorities as well as citizens.
GE	Shang & Price, 2019	Education – success factor	Education and Literacy	The success of the Georgia project was the result of two crucial elements – education and data quality.
GE	Shang & Price, 2019	Education – success factor	Education and Literacy	For a Blockchain-based project to succeed, all stakeholders must be educated about Blockchain technology and the challenges it can address. Tomicah Tillemann, founder of the Blockchain Trust Accelerator, said of the Georgia project that "education and public engagement are as crucial as the technical side of the work. Technology is not going to take care of itself. People and the government need to know why they are using this technology and what problem it can solve." Throughout the project, the NAPR helped the Georgian people understand how Blockchain technology can ensure the immutability of land title data without sacrificing privacy
GE	Aarvik, 2024	Importance of e-government – success factor	Government, Control and Cooperation	A developed e-Government service is a prerequisite.
GE	Lazuashvili et al., 2019	Importance of e-government – success factor	Government, Control and Cooperation	Having a developed e-government is one of the biggest benefits to face the challenge of blockchain adoption. This element is also identified as a major support factor for the successful implementation of the Georgian land-titling project. Based on international rankings, Georgia shows significant results in the advancement of e-government development as also previously also discussed in the extended version of this paper.
GE	Aarvik, 2024	Vital Public-private cooperation – success factor	Government, Control and Cooperation	Sustained public-private partnership was beneficial in Georgia.
GE	Lazuashvili et al., 2019	Vital Public-private cooperation – success factor	Government, Control and Cooperation	Public-private partnership is a crucial aspect for blockchain-technology adoption. In case of Georgia, the Bitfury group develops the blockchain solution for the government and since then keeps providing the service. The same applies to other adopter countries as well where occasionally even several privatesector companies provide the solutions for integrating blockchain technology into existing land-registry systems.
GE	Lazuashvili et al., 2019	Vital Public-private cooperation – success factor	Government, Control and Cooperation	Besides the aspiration for Gerogia to portray a high e-governance development standard, reducing project risk for the government by initiating public-private cooperation is identified as a major incentive. Additionally, in the Georgian case, costs of

ISO	Source	Descriptive Code	Thematic Code	Segment
GE	Lazuashvili et al., 2019	Vital public-private cooperation – success factor	Government, Control and Cooperation	(continued from page 92) the project along with the technology maintenance expenditures are covered by the private blockchain service-provider company.
GE	Aarvik, 2024	Blockchain legal framework necessary	Legal and Regulatory Framework	A developed legal framework was necessary for moving 'blockchainisation' of land titles past the pilot stage.
GE	v. Weizsäcker et al., 2018	Legal limitations smart contracts	Legal and Regulatory Framework	Secondly, the legal status of smart contracts still needs to be specified, possibly requiring 4 legal amendments of contract law, along with the changing role of the institution of the land registry. In addition, questions regarding data sovereignty are likely to arise, particularly with regards to varying privacy and data-hosting laws across different countries. Data privacy concerns may be addressed by employing cryptographic methods such as zeroknowledge proofs.
GE	Lazuashvili et al., 2019	Legislative framework regarding data – success factor	Legal and Regulatory Framework	The legislative framework is a crucial aspect for the successful integration of blockchain technology. In case of Georgia, the project success is greatly determined by the flexibility of the respective regulations that do not hinder NAPR from saving the citizens' data on the blockchain. In cases of other countries such as Sweden or The Netherlands, for administering blockchain technology into the public service, major regulatory changes are required.
GE	Lazuashvili et al., 2019	Further legislative research	Legal and Regulatory Framework	In the case of the Georgian government, one of the respondents admits that after the completion of the pilot project of the land titling "blockchainisation", NAPR sees the need for conducting research about the legislative framework of Georgia for supporting the further development of this blockchain project.
GE	Shang & Price, 2019	Institutional legal support	Legal and Regulatory Framework	The high quality of the NAPR data was a consequence of the political reforms pursued by the Republic of Georgia before the project. This speaks to an important truth of Blockchain-based solutions for governments: while the technology can ensure the security and immutability of information, it cannot be a substitute for the institutional infrastructure that is essential for ensuring the quality of data.
GE	v. Weizsäcker et al., 2018	Technical limitations smart contracts	Technical Limitations	The small-scale solution of timestamping transactions of existing land registries by writing hashes on a public ledger is relatively straightforward and easy to implement. Yet, the more disruptive solution in which land transactions are executed in a fully automated manner through the use of smart contracts, faces significant implementation hurdles
GE	v. Weizsäcker et al., 2018	Technical limitations smart contracts	Technical Limitations	Firstly, land titles and obligations are often complex and involve additional information beyond the identity of the land tenant. For instance, mechanisms and procedures have to be defined for land seizure in cases of insolvency etc. Projecting such complex modalities of rules and obligations into a blockchain will require not only careful and thorough coding of smart contracts but also institutions to go through a significant adaptation of their management processes.

Appendix 2

ISO	Source	Descriptive Code	Thematic Code	Segment
GE	v. Weizsäcker et al., 2018	Lack of block-chain maturity	Technical Limitations	Another hurdle relates to the lack of maturity of blockchain technology. Public blockchains are a phenomenon of the past 10 years, while land titles are meant to be kept for up to 100 years or more.
GE	Aarvik, 2024	Public perception / trust in institutions	Trust and Perception	This, perhaps, explains why public perceptions around corruption have not continued to improve since blockchain was added to the registry.
GE	Aarvik, 2024	Public perception / trust in institutions	Trust and Perception	showed that public mistrust of politicians remained, when it came to influence over land transactions.
GE	Aarvik, 2024	Public perception / trust in institutions	Trust and Perception	As we have seen, trust in the institutions handling the land registry is crucial; trust in the blockchain security layer, less so.

Authors

Pablo L. Reiser is a graduate of the Master of Science in Real Estate (MScRE) programme at the Lucerne University of Applied Sciences and Arts (HSLU). He also holds a Bachelor of Science in International Hospitality Business Management from EHL Hospitality Business School (CH) and a Master of Science in International Banking and Finance from Lingnan University (HK).

He has gained international professional experience in the hospitality industry in Japan and Singapore, as well as in the banking sector in Switzerland, where he has worked in client account management and asset management. His career path reflects a broad international outlook and an interdisciplinary focus on finance, banking, and real assets.

His research interests lie at the intersection of real estate, finance, and innovation. His MScRE thesis explores the barriers and success factors in implementing blockchain-based land registries across different international contexts, contributing to the ongoing academic discussion on the digital transformation of real estate markets.

P. L. Reiser et al., *Blockchain in Global Land Registries*, https://doi.org/10.1007/978-3-658-50076-4

Prof. Dr. Michael Truebestein FRICS is professor of real estate management and investments as well as Head of the Master of Science in Real Estate (MScRE)-program at Lucerne University (HSLU). Furthermore, he was elected president of the RICS in Switzerland in 2019.

He studied international business administration at the EBS University of Economics and Law (D) and wrote his Ph.D. Thesis at the University of Regensburg (D). He was appointed professor of real estate management at the University of Kufstein (A) for 5 years (2008–2013). Since 2013 he has been working as a professor of real estate investment and management at Lucerne University/HSLU (CH).

Michael Truebestein is author of various publications in the area of real estate strategies, (international) real estate investments, asset management, real estate markets and digitization. In 2014, he initiated the annual study on "Real Estate Investments and Asset Management" of institutional investors (in cooperation with the ASIP / Swiss Pension Fund Association) and carried out the world's first tokenization of a property in 2019, the "Hello World" in Baar (CH). He serves as a member of the board of directors for an international real estate investment company. In 2021, 2022 and 2023, the Swiss media elected him as one of the 100 most influential and important personalities in the Swiss real estate industry.

Dr. oec. HSG Matthias Daniel Aepli is a lecturer at Lucerne University (HSLU) and an entrepreneur in the real estate sector.

He studied business administration with a major in finance at the university of northwestern Switzerland (FHNW). At the University of St. Gallen (HSG) he completed the Master of Arts program in banking and finance and received his Ph.D. with his thesis in quantitative finance. Matthias Daniel Aepli is author of various publications in the area of real estate management, investment strategies, asset management, corporate financial management and risk management.

Since 2012 Matthias Daniel Aepli has been working as a lecturer of corporate finance, risk management and real estate management at Lucerne University (HSLU) (CH). In addition to his work in academia, he serves as a member of the board of directors and is a renowned serial entrepreneur in the field of real estate.

The manufacturer's authorised representative in the EU is Springer Nature Customer Service Centre GmbH, Europaplatz 3, 69115 Heidelberg, Germany. If you have any concerns regarding our products, please contact ProductSafety@springernature.com

Printed and bound by CPI Group (UK) Ltd, Croydon, CR0 4YY
04/05/2026
02102364-0002